D1176902

SABOR!

A Guide to Tropical Fruits and Vegetables and Central American Foods

By Carolina Avila and Marilyn Root
Illustrated by Carolina Avila

641.5   Root, Marilyn
A-958s   ¡SABOR! A Guide to Tropical Fruits &
          Vegetables and Central American Foods /
          Carolina Avila and Marilyn Root. -- San José :
          Litografía e Imprenta LIL, 1997.
               224 p. : il. ; 22.8 cm.

               ISBN 9977-47-226-2

               1. Recetarios. I. Avila, Carolina, coautor. II.
          Título.

Ilustrated by: *Carolina Avila*

Printed in Costa Rica by:
Litografía e Imprenta LIL, S.A.
Tel. (506) 235-0011

TABLE OF CONTENTS

PREFACE

After a long career as an educator in the San Francisco Bay Area, I pulled up stakes and moved to Costa Rica in 1991. One of the first things I noticed was the wide array of fresh fruits and vegetables in supermarkets and at *ferias del agricultor* (open air farmers' markets). There were many I had never seen before and had no clue as to how to prepare them yet alone make dishes utilizing them!

From my situation emerged the idea for this guide. I wanted to learn more about the tropical fruits and vegetables found in Central America. As a new resident, I also experienced difficulty choosing items in the supermarket. I didn't know the names for some meat cuts and poultry parts. Although some packaged items had labels in English, many did not.

Part of knowing a "culture" is becoming familiar with its food. Newcomers and visitors to Central America will not fully experience the region unless they learn something about regional produce and cooking.

I have always enjoyed sampling various ethnic cuisines. One of my hobbies while living in Marin County, California was to journey into The City to try small San Francisco ethnic restaurants. Since my move to Costa Rica, I have had the opportunity to write restaurant reviews for the *Tico Times*. In the process, I have learned more about regional cooking, but, frankly, my knowledge has been limited. Thus, the process of compiling information for this book has been a learning experience for me.

Several years back, when I visited an Escazú souvenir shop and art gallery, *El Sabor Tico*, I met the young Salvadorian owner, Carolina Avila. Carolina had been educated in California where she met and married a "gringo". She lived in Santa Barbara, California for a number of years prior to moving to Costa Rica in 1990. Since *El Sabor Tico* carries tourist oriented items, I asked Carolina how marketable this type of book might be. She was enthused about the idea...and offered to be my collaborator! I have researched the information for the guide and have done the writing, but Carolina has provided the illustrations and most of the recipes, translating a number of them from their original Spanish.

Some of our recipe selections are regional favorites, but others are "gringo-ized" versions of Latin dishes designed to appeal to North American and European palates. Still other recipes are included because they utilize the tropical fruits and vegetables we feature, but are hardly "*tipico*" dishes prepared in Central American homes.

English language cookbooks with Central American recipes have been written, but to our knowledge no one has written anything to assist with the identification of unfamiliar fruits and vegetables or with the selection and purchase of food products in general. We think this book can help our readers to prepare some interesting dishes and will be of assistance to them when shopping at the market and when ordering restaurant meals.

Once we undertook our tasks, we experienced some difficulty locating good information. We have gathered bits and pieces of information from a variety of sources. The references we have utilized are listed near the end of our guide. However, there are individuals who have helped us whom we wish to acknowledge. We thank Jorge Gonzales for providing materials which helped in the writing of the fruit section and Mary Alice Lesko for supplying us with her collection of "What is it?" columns. Among others, we are indebted to Lorena Di Tolla, Gloria Dubois, Lizette Lacombe, Heidi Landon, Liliana Larragán, Isabel Matheson, Vida Raven, and Silvia Silva who have shared recipes with us. A special thanks to Robin Emigh of Robin's Specialty Desserts. All these contributors have made our guide a truly "international" endeavor!

Finally, we wish to express our appreciation to Noreen Liptak, Bill Fischer, and Ronald Maingot who have taken time to proof-read our work. We are thrilled that two men had the interest!

Our guide takes its title in part from the name of Carolina's shop, *El Sabor Tico*, but also because *Sabor!* translates as "'Taste!" We expect our book to appeal to people with discriminating "taste" who enjoy sampling new foods. Whether you, our reader, are a tourist, a Central American resident, or someone of another stripe, we hope you find our publication useful. *Buen Provecho!*

Marilyn Root
May 1997

8

INTRODUCTION

This book is dedicated to the gringa who asked her maid to put the *sopa,* thinking it was soap, in the washing machine and then had a terrible mess on her hands! Even though the maid thought her employer *un poco loca* (a little crazy), the dutiful employee did as she was told and added soup to the wash!

Believe it or not this is a more or less true story related by a North American newcomer to Costa Rica. We are certain every non-Spanish speaking newcomer and visitor to our region can relate a comparable tale or two. Amusing situations occur in restaurants as well. English speakers think they are ordering one thing, then their dish turns out to be something entirely different! Even if you know some Spanish, you cannot rely on literal translations. To provide a simple illustration, *gallo pinto*, the Costa Rican national dish, translates as "speckled rooster", yet it's a tasty white rice and bean dish. *Sopa,* usually means soup as we know it, but there are also *sopas secas* (dry soups) which are rice dishes.

Predicaments like these seem humorous in retrospect, but at the time such situations were stressful and exasperating. One of the greatest pleasures of living and traveling in a foreign country is encountering new foods and dining experiences. We want our reader to make the most of his culinary adventures during his stay in Central America.

Those choosing to come to Costa Rica will find some appealing circumstances. Unlike in México and most other Central American countries, the water is potable. This means you do not have to boil it or treat it, just take it from the tap and use it to cook or to drink. For this reason, all ice is usually safe, too. However, one should exercise some caution when venturing outside the Central Valley. It's always best to ask about the quality of the water! For those who are skeptical about our remarks and really want to be safe and secure, you can buy plastic bottles of *agua pura* at the supermarket.

Another advantage you will discover is you do not have to treat raw fruits and vegetables, just rinse them before eating! Treatment with water mixed with a few drops of clorox (*cloro*) or by some other method is not necessary in Costa Rica, but you need to be careful in other parts of Central America. To be safe, some like to peel all raw fruits and to cook all vegetables. In truth, we can say we have experienced food poisoning and upset stomachs more frequently in the States than here in Costa Rica!

A good rule of thumb when visiting a place is: if it looks clean, chances are the food and water are okay! When dining in restaurants, if you are unable to peek into the kitchen, a visit to the bathroom will give you a good idea as to the cleanliness of the establishment. The reader will observe standards of cleanliness are high in Costa Rica!

One of our concerns is the use of powerful insecticides in Central American agriculture. Organically grown products are beginning to be introduced into supermarkets, but toxic pesticides are widely used. It's likely items purchased in supermarkets or consumed raw in first class restaurants will be okay, but you may want to take a little extra caution with items purchased elsewhere. *"Tipico"* restaurants and *sodas* (similiar to "coffee shops" in the States) often do not have good refrigeration systems, thus sometimes foodstuffs are left standing out longer than they should. Just as you would in your own country, don't eat anything that smells bad or doesn't look fresh! Practice "When in doubt, throw it out!"

Another discovery we have made is that many dishes are laced with MSG. It is not only used in Chinese restaurants, but is often an ingredient in *gallo pinto* and other dishes. A number of places use MSG as a meat tenderizer! Those who choose to avoid it, can request their meals prepared "*sin ajinomoto*", without MSG!

Many come to Costa Rica with preconceived notions about Costa Rican cuisine. The expectation is of hot and spicy food like Mexican cuisine. Visitors will find rice and beans to be a large part of the Costa Rican diet, but they will not find their food spicy. Most Costa Rican dishes are actually quite bland.

One of the most common Costa Rican plates is the *casado*, a small portion of beef, fish, or chicken accompanied by *gallo pinto,* a cabbage salad, and perhaps potatoes or a vegetable. Chances are the meat served as a part of the *casado* will be pan fried as will be the chicken or fish, but the latter two could also be prepared *empanizadas* (breaded).

Many plates in Costa Rica contain two and sometimes even three starches. Usually one of the starches is white rice, but others can be boiled potatoes, sweet potatoes, plantain, yuca or another tropical tuber. In Italian restaurants we sometimes see potatoes served along with pasta, and french fries (*papas fritas*) can accompany Chinese meals!

On "typical plates" mixed green salads are almost unknown. The meal is usually accompanied by a cabbage salad (*ensalada de repollo*), or, at best, a couple of slices of tomato on a bed of lettuce. Many Costa Ricans do not eat lettuce and raw vegetables. Perhaps their avoidance dates back to a period when one could not count on the safety of consuming raw produce.

If a vegetable accompanies your meal, chances are it will be too overcooked for your taste. Vegetables are typically boiled rather than steamed or sautéed. Historically, there may be good reason to overcook, but today it seems unnecessary.

Just about as popular as the *casado* is *olla de carne* and *arroz con pollo* or *arroz con camarones.* Word-for-word, *olla de carne* means "pot of meat". It is basically a beef stew served in a oversized soup bowl. The cook puts in just about any vegetable good for stewing along with starches such as pieces of potato or yuca. The *arroz* dishes border on being similar to Chinese-style fried rice. Your plate usually contains nothing more than a large mound of rice seasoned with annatto, chopped onion, green or red pepper, and herbs with either small shrimp or chicken morsels added. We like Costa Rican *picadillos,* literally "chopped dishes", as they are nicely seasoned combinations of various diced vegetables and starches, sometimes including ground meat. They can be eaten as a main course or as a side dish.

Guanacaste is the Texas of Costa Rica. This region produces some very fine beef. When in the market, look for good quality cuts. Steak is reasonably priced, and there are many restaurants which specialize in barbecued steaks grilled over wood (*a la leña*), giving

11

them a much finer flavor than when grilled over charcoal. To enhance the steak, it is not uncommon to have *chirmol* (Mexican sauce) or *chimichurri* (Argentine sauce) served as an accompaniment. Since most Ticos prefer their meat well done, even if you ask for your meat rare, you are apt to find it only on the pink side!

As in other Central American countries, corn is the backbone of Costa Rican cooking. Tortillas made from cornmeal are served with "*tipico*" meals. A cornmeal, called *masa*, is utilized to make tamales which are especially popular at Christmas. Included in our book are sections on both making tortillas and preparing tamales.

The Costa Ricans love pizza and pasta...are these Latin foods? Many "*tipico*" restaurants serve pasta dishes, especially spaghetti plates. Pizza comes with the traditional toppings, but it is not uncommon to find toppings foreign to your palette.

Not only do pizza parlors abound, but places serving hamburgers as well. Many Central Americans who like to embrace American products have the conception that the hamburger is the national food of the United States! Some of us may not be all that enamored with the hamburger, but just go by a Burger King or MacDonalds on Sunday and you will find entire Tico families out for a special treat.

AT THE MARKET...

The fresh fruits and vegetables featured in this book can be purchased in many locations. Supermarkets like Automercado, Periferico, Rayo Azul, and Más x Menos can be counted on to have fresh items free of pests, but not always of pesticides. Supermarkets are also the most costly places to buy fresh fruits and vegetables. Frequently, the products are packaged in cellophane with enough items to feed an army! However, we have found most places will accommodate and open the package for those who desire less. Additionally, the supermarkets stock imported or hard to find items like fresh peaches, apples, asparagus, and artichokes. If you cannot find an item at Yaohan or Saretto, the country's most elite supermarkets, be assured, you cannot find it in Costa Rica!

12

One of the real delights in Central America is to visit a weekend *feria del agricultor* (farmer's market). *Ferias* are usually held on Saturday or Sunday morning in neighborhoods and in most small towns where a street is sectioned off and farmers set up stands. Each Saturday morning, *La Nacion*, the county's leading newspaper, has a column indicating the prices you can expect to find at *ferias* this weekend. The column also gives shoppers an idea as to which fruits and vegetables are in season and available. The prices at *ferias* are very fair--often half the amount found in the supermarket. The produce is the freshest you can find, and the vendors are honest. On occasion we have had vendors return change when we overpaid!

It's best to come early to the *feria* while the selection is good and the morning sun not too hot. Arm yourself with a large sack or a box on your luggage cart as you surely will buy more than you expected. Small handwritten signs name the item and the price. You can utilize the vocabulary lists at the back of this book for your shopping. Prices are listed by the kilo (2.2 pounds), but you can buy a *medio* (half) kilo or a *cuarto* (fourth) kilo. Some foodstuffs will have the letters *c/u*, meaning *cada una* (each one). You may see the words *sazón* or *tierno* after the fruit or vegetable you plan to purchase. They merely refer to the degree of ripeness. For example, *Zapallo sazón* is a mature squash while *zapallo tierno* is young or green. In addition to fresh produce, plants, flowers, baskets, and other items are sold.

There is a large public market taking up several blocks in downtown San José. It borders on Avenidas Central and 1 and Calles 6 and 8. Lots of stalls dominate the area, selling everything you could possibly need from cooking utensils to bakery products, to meat, fish, and poultry. All items are reasonably priced, but one needs to be a selective shopper. The quality of some items is not good and some agricultural and meat products do not appear to be very fresh. Refrigeration is not always used. The area abounds with pick-pockets, so be careful with your money and possessions. Those of us who live here prefer the neighborhood ferias to the Central Market, but the *Mercado* can be an interesting morning experience for the tourist.

Costa Rica also is saturated with *mini-supers* and *pulperías*. They are neighborhood convenience stores,

13

the equivalent of 7/11's in the United States. These stores stock produce, meat and poultry, and sometimes even deli items, but often their freshness is questionable. We tend to utilize them as we did convenience stores in the States, as quick stops for beverages, a newspaper, or for packaged goods.

Finally, it's fun to buy produce and dairy products when traveling through the countryside. Roadside vendors are always *muy amable* (very friendly) and their foodstuffs are fresh. Roadside products may be of superior quality, or, although fresh, may be inferior to the same products found in town. Prices are not necessarily any cheaper than at the *feria*, but if the price is a little high, you can often bargain. A delightful time can be had sampling cheese or fresh *natilla* (sour cream) at a dairy on the way to Irazu Volcano or honey from a beekeeper encountered on a trip through the San Carlos Valley.

To assist you, our guide provides a list of Spanish names for common North American food products. Illustrations of various cuts of meat are included in the guide as well as Spanish vocabulary lists for a variety of meats, seafoods, fish, and poultry products.

IN THE RESTAURANT...

One can eat in a wide variety of restaurants in Costa Rica. There are Italian, Chinese, German, Swiss, French, and Japanese restaurants as well as restaurants featuring Peruvian and Argentinean food. Usually the menus at these international restaurants are written in both Spanish and English. The menus in neighborhood restaurants and "tipico" restaurants, which do not cater to tourists, are apt to be in Spanish only. Again, lists at the end of our guide will assist you, if you need help reading menus.

Usually a restaurant menu is divided into several sections. *Entradas* or *Entremeses* are first courses or hors d'oeurves. *Ensaladas* and *Sopas* are almost self-explanatory as they have more or less equivalent names in English. *Platos Fuertes*, literally meaning strong plates, are main courses. In most restaurants, the *Plato Fuerte* is large enough that a diner with an average appetite does not need to order anything additional.

14

The *Plato Fuerte* usually has a starch and a vegetable-- and sometimes two vegetables or two starches and a small salad!   Since portions are very ample in Costa Rica, if there are *entradas, ensaladas* or *sopas* on the menu which you find intriguing, we suggest you order two of them and skip the *plato fuerte*.   Big eaters may want to "go for broke" and have a first course, entree, and dessert.   A list of desserts (*postres*) and drinks (*bebidas*) usually rounds out the restaurant menu.

Readers should be acquainted with some customs encountered when dining out.   Often we have seen Costa Ricans eating some delectable dishes and have inquired as to which item it is on the menu, only to be told, "It's not on the menu"! If they have the ingredients on hand, a good number of chefs will prepare a meal to suit your tastes.   This is especially true when preparing pasta. For example, if you are ordering *espagetti marinera*, (spagetti with seafood) you can ask to have the dish prepared without any seafood item to which you have an aversion.   Or, if you would like a fresh tomato sauce rather than a cream sauce, just ask! If a salad is included on the *plato fuerte* and you are tired of the traditional cabbage salad, try requesting lettuce and tomato with vinegar and oil.

At lunch, a number of restaurants have economically priced weekday specials. They may be named *Menu Ejecutivo, Menu del Día, Plato del Día* or some similar term.   Some are just an entree, but many include a drink and a dessert or even a first course. The problem is some restaurants fail to list these specials or forget to insert notice of them into the menu, but usually the daily special is listed on a chalkboard near the restaurant's entrance.   The "special" can be announced in Spanish only; thus, it always pays to ask if the place has one!

We have also had the experience of visiting ethnic restaurants where we were not given every menu. Chinese and Japanese restaurants frequently have speciality menus written in Chinese or Japanese which they provide only to Oriental patrons.   The moral: if you speak Spanish or the language of the restaurant owner, inquire about additional menus!   On a couple of occasions, we have found better prices on Spanish language menus than on English menus. If you speak Spanish and the menu you are given is in English only, ask to see the Spanish menu! Descriptions of dishes will likely be better on Spanish menus...we have viewed some inaccurate and amusing translations!

Most Central Americans eat their principal meal at lunch. Costa Rica is a country of "morning people", so those who rise at dawn are hungry by mid-day! A "sweet" or snack shared with friends and family is customary to many in the late afternoon. In the evening, often not until eight or nine, a second fairly substantial meal may be taken. We find this a sensible way to eat and try to follow the Ticos. On special occasions or weekends, we may reverse our pattern and dine in the evening as we would in the States. In the Tico household, it is not uncommon to find a large pot on the stove all day. As family members come and go, they help themselves to their daily hot meal.

When it comes to tipping, Costa Rican restaurants differ from those in many countries. A 10% tip is always included on the check, so you need not give an extra sum unless some special service was provided. In addition, there is a high government tax on all food served in restaurants--13%. This means nearly one fourth of your meal check goes toward something other than food! Ouch! However, travelers will find some places in the countryside incorporate the tax into the price of the meal.

Visitors and new residents should be aware of still another custom. The check (*la cuenta*) is never given to you until you ask for it! You could find yourself waiting until closing time if you expect the waiter to automatically bring it! On the other hand, it is comforting to feel the management is not rushing you to leave. A nice touch at better restaurants is a waiter or doorman with an umbrella to escort you in and out during a rain storm. If you travel to a restaurant by car, many restaurants have guarded parking. A small *propina* (tip) for the attendant is expected. We find only a very few restaurants serve water with meals, but will bring it if you request it. Dining out at places with good food and reasonable prices is one of the pleasures of being in Costa Rica!

AT HOME...

Should you decide to take up residence in Costa Rica, even if it is temporary residence in a small furnished apartment or an aparthotel, you will need to stock the kitchen. One kitchen item you will find to be absolutely essential is a blender (*licuadora*). Without it you will not be able to prepare many of our recipes. Other standard kitchen items, such as graters, peelers, ladles, and wire whisks, can be purchased at most supermarkets, and some hardware stores which stock household goods. CEMACO and Home Mart are excellent stores to visit for a good selection of quality household goods as well as hardware items.

You will find many stoves in Costa Rica with oven temperatures given in centigrade rather than fahrenheit, thus we include a handy temperature conversion chart. Usually measuring cups can be located with metric measurements and their American equivalents, but if you do not have them, we provide simple conversion tables for those unfamiliar with the metric system.

One of the treasures of Costa Rica are the *refrescos naturales*--the host of natural drinks made from fresh fruit. We want to teach you how to make a few of them. Other delicious tropical drinks, with or without alcohol, can be made. Since this is "coffee country" even non-coffee drinkers may want to try some of our guide's coffee drinks. Finally, our "Central American Classics" section contains many traditional dishes to sample. Read on and enjoy with *Sabor!*

ANNATTO/ACHIOTE

Not many North Americans are familiar with achiote, annatto in English, but it is a food coloring heavily utilized in Latin American and Caribbean cooking. Achiote is not an herb, but the seed of a fruit native to tropical America, *bixa orellana*.

Achiote grows on a pretty little tree, sometimes known as the Lipstick tree because it bears vibrant pink flowers. The fruit is capsule-shaped, covered with soft thorns, and contains a seed pod with triangular rust colored seeds. The dye is extracted from these seeds.

Achiote has been cultivated and used in Central America since pre-Columbian times. Pre-Columbian indians used it to decorate their bodies, clothing, and utensils. Because of its rich golden hue, today achiote is used commercially to color butter, margarine, cheese, and other foods.

Central American cooks are never without achiote in their homes in the way we northerners are never without salt and pepper! In Costa Rica you have likely eaten achiote many times without realizing it. It's added

18

to just about anything which could benefit from a little color! Principally, achiote is used to give a golden tint to rice, chicken and pork dishes, and to soups. Not only does achiote color, it mildly flavors, possessing an earthy aroma which hints of paprika.

The proper way to use achiote is to buy the seeds at the *Mercado Central* and grind them to extract the dye! However, most often achiote is purchased in a paste form at the supermarket or bought powdered in cellophane wrapped packages. Try experimenting with it! It's a cheap alternative to saffron!

ANNATTO OIL
Aceite de Achiote

1 cup vegetable oil or light olive oil
1/2 cup of annatto seeds

Heat the oil in a heavy saucepan over a medium heat. Add the annatto seeds and cook until the oil is reddish gold and the seeds begin to crackle, about 3 minutes. Cool and strain the oil into a clean container with a lid.

Use annatto oil for frying onions, browning pork or chicken, or for perking up salad dressings. Stored in a jar it will keep for months, even at room temperature. Be careful not to spill it as the orange stains are murder to remove from clothing.
Makes: 1 cup

ANNATTO SAUCE
Salsa de Achiote

1 1/2 cups chopped onion	4 T. lime juice
1/2 cup chopped green pimento stuffed olives	1 T. ground annatto powder
	1 tsp. ground coriander
1 large green pepper, minced	1 cup fresh orange juice
1/4 cup olive oil	

Heat the olive oil and saute the onion until it is translucent. Add the chopped olives and bell pepper. Cook 5 minutes, stirring as needed. Add the other ingredients and simmer covered at a low heat for 10 minutes.

This sauce can be poured over sauteed boneless chicken breasts or pork chops. It is wonderful with fish fillets. For fish, place the uncooked fillets in a Pyrex baking dish and pour the sauce over them. Bake for about 20 minutes in a 350°F oven.

Serves: 6 to 8

CHICKEN AND TORTILLA CASSEROLE
Cacerola de Pollo y Tortilla

2 large onions, minced	2 cans tomato paste (4-6 oz.)
1 tsp. achiote powder	3 large tomatoes, seeded and
4 packages tortillas	pureed with 1/2 cup water
2 cups milk or half and half	and the tomato paste
1 bunch cilantro, chopped	1 cup Mozzarella or
1 1/2 cups chicken broth	Monterey Jack, grated
3 cloves garlic, minced	1 cup Cheddar cheese, grated
5 green peppers, cut into strips	1 large chicken, cooked and
3 T. cooking oil	cubed

Heat the cooking oil and saute the garlic, green pepper, and onion with the achiote powder. When caramelized, add the cubed chicken, mix well, and simmer covered for 10 minutes. Add the tomato sauce mixture and the chicken broth. Mix well, and simmer for 15 minutes. When finished add the cooked and cubed chicken.

Meanwhile, grease a 9 x 13 inch Pyrex baking dish. Heat the tortillas to soften them, and cut each into 4 strips. In the baking dish, put a layer of tortillas followed by half of the two cheeses, and 1 cup of half and half. Top it with half of the chicken/tomato sauce. Repeat the process, finishing with a layer of tortilla strips and the remaining cheese on top. Bake in a 325°F oven for 20 to 25 minutes until hot and bubbly.

Serves: 8 to 10

POTATO HASH
Picadillo de Papa

2 lbs. potatoes
1/2 lb. ground beef
1/2 lb. pork sausage, without
   casings
1 medium onion, chopped
2 garlic cloves, minced
1/2 to 3/4 cup chicken broth

1 tsp. ground cumin
1 bunch cilantro, chopped
1 green pepper, chopped
1/2 stick butter or margarine
3 T. cooking oil
1 tsp. annatto paste or
   1/2 tsp. annatto powder

Peel and cube the raw potatoes. Parboil the potato cubes for 4 minutes in salted boiling water. Remove and drain.

Fry the beef and sausage, and set aside. In another pan, heat the cooking oil and butter. Saute the onion, pepper, achiote, garlic, and the drained potatoes for about 10 minutes, stirring frequently.

Add the cooked beef and sausage along with the chicken broth. Cover and simmer until the potatoes are cooked and the liquid is absorbed. Serve with tortillas.

Serves: 6 to 8

CHICKEN WITH YELLOW RICE
Arroz con Pollo

1 large chicken (about 4 lbs.),
   cut into 8-even size pieces
1 tsp. dried oregano

1 tsp. ground cumin
1/2 tsp. white pepper
1 T. red wine vinegar

Broth:
2 T. annatto oil (see above recipe)
1 small onion, finely chopped
1 small red sweet pepper, cored,
   seeded, and finely chopped
3 cloves garlic, minced
3 T. finely chopped cilantro
1 small tomato, seeded and diced
Salt and pepper to taste

3 cups water
1 cup dry white wine
1 1/2 cups of beer
1/2 tsp. annatto seeds
1 T. tomato paste
1/2 cup pimento-stuffed
   green olives

To finish the dish:
1 lb. Valencia, Arborio, or other
   short grain rice
2 red peppers, diced

1/2 cup canned petits pois
   (tiny green peas)

21

Wash the chicken and blot it dry with paper towels. Mix the oregano, cumin, white pepper, and vinegar in a large bowl. Add the chicken, turning the pieces to cover with the mixture. Let marinate for 15 minutes.

Heat the annatto oil in a large heat proof casserole. Brown the chicken pieces all over, about 2 minutes per side. Transfer the chicken to a platter and pour out all but 2 tablespoons of the fat.

Add the onion, bell pepper, garlic, and cilantro and cook over a medium heat until soft, but not brown, 1 to 2 minutes. Add the tomato and cook for 1 minute more. Return the chicken to the casserole and cook for 1 additional minute.

Add the water, wine, beer, tomato paste, olives, and salt and pepper. Bring the mixture to a boil. Reduce the heat, cover, and gently simmer the chicken for 30 minutes.

While the chicken is cooking, place the annatto seeds in a small saucepan with 1/4 cup of the chicken cooking liquid. Gently simmer for 5 minutes. Strain the mixture back into the chicken. (The recipe can be prepared ahead to this stage.)

Finish the dish: Thoroughly wash the rice until the water runs clear of starch. Thirty minutes before serving, bring the chicken mixture to a boil. Stir in the rice, reduce the heat, cover the pan, and gently simmer the rice until tender, 20 to 25 minutes. If the rice starts to dry out, add more water. If the mixture looks too soupy, remove the cover during the last 5 minutes of cooking.

Just before the rice is finished, stir in half of the petits pois and diced red peppers Use the remainder to garnish the top and serve at once.

Serves: 6 to 8

ANNONA/ANONA

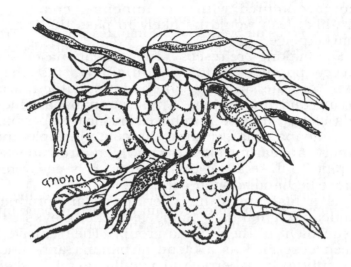

anona

Annonas (Two n's in English, one in Spanish) are a group of 60 or more tropical fruits believed to be native to the Inter-Andean valleys of Ecuador, Colombia and Peru. Many anonnas, such as the prized cherimoya, grow in the cooler temperatures of the tropical highlands while others like the guanábana flourish in lowland areas. Many names are applied to the various annona species, often erroneously.

Four annona species are typically found in Latin America. In Costa Rica, the anonna or custard apple, *A. reticulata*, is abundant along with the guanábana, *A. muricata*, known to English speakers by the dreadful name, soursop. The cherimoya, *A. cherimola*, and a cherimoya hybrid can sometimes be purchased while the atemoya, *A. squamosa*, is not available.

All members of the annona group have a white, sweet, pineapple-flavored pulp. The pulp is more savory in some, like the cherimoya, than in others. The pulp is usually eaten raw or used to prepare fresh fruit drinks. Annonas are also used to flavor ice cream and custards.

The anona (Span.) or custard apple (Eng.) is the "ugly duckling" of the species. It is a heart shaped fruit usually about 3 to 6 inches in diameter. Its growth is often lopsided or irregular; the skin is light green, but begins to discolor and blacken when ripe. Those who are not acquainted with the annona's creamy white, custard-like flesh would be likely to pass the fruit up in the marketplace.

For making "refrescos", the guanábana or soursop is a very popular fruit. Additionally, it's the only member of the family which lends itself well to preserving and processing. Thus, guanábana jellies and spreads can readily be purchased in local supermarkets. The guanábana is larger than the custard apple and has a leathery appearing skin from which protrude stubby soft "spines". Like all in this species, it is easily bruised and must be handled with care.

As a highland fruit, cherimoyas are produced in the Andean highlands. Some feel cherimoyas are the most succulent of the annona group. Their elusive flavor has been described as a blend of banana and pineapple with a subtle strawberry and vanilla taste! *Qué rica!* Cherimoyas have become a prized import to the United States where they sell for as much as $4 to $5 a pound! They are not often found in Costa Rica.

The atermoya or sugar apple is a hybrid species, a cross between the annona and the cherimoya. It grows in tropical or near tropical climates, but is rarely seen here. Since they are very similar, sometimes the distinction in not made between the atemoya and the annona.

All the fruits in the annona family should be picked while still firm and allowed to soften at room temperature. To test for ripeness, apply soft pressure. If the fruit gives, it's ripe! These fruits are best used very fresh, as ripe fruit will deteriorate quickly; however, they can be stored in the refrigerator for a few days, or the pulp can be frozen.

ANNONA PASTRY CREAM
Crema de Anona

1 cup annona pulp   1 egg yolk
1 1/2 cup milk   2 T. sugar
2 T. corn starch

Purée the annona pulp and 1/2 cup of milk in a blender, and set aside.

In a sauce pan, heat the remaining cup milk and add sugar. Mix the egg yolk and cornstarch in a small mixing bowl, then add it to the milk and sugar mixture just before it boils. Reduce the heat and stir constantly until the mixture thickens.

Remove from the heat, let cool, and add the annona. This pastry cream can be used over chocolate ice cream or served with crepes or pound cake.
Makes: 2 cups
Good!

GUANABANA CAKE
Queque de Guanábana

Cake:
1 package of yellow cake mix   1/2 cup of light rum

Frosting:
2 lbs. guanábana pulp, seeded   1 8 oz. can condensed milk
3/4 cup whipping cream

Prepare the cake according to the package instructions. Make in two 9-inch layer pans. Sprinkle the layers with the rum and set aside.

Separate the seeds from the guanábana pulp. Put the pulp, condensed milk, and whipping cream into a blender or a food processor.   Mix well to a whipped consistency.

Spread the guanábana mixture between the layers and on top as a frosting. Refrigerate for a least 2 hours before serving or overnight. Serve the cake cold.
Serves: 8 to 10

AVOCADO/AGUACATE

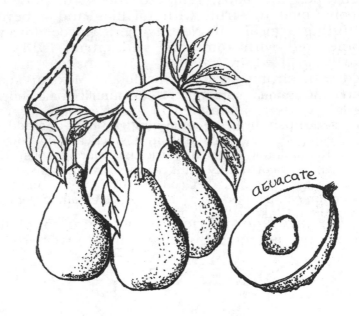

aguacate

Yes, the avocado is a fruit, not a vegetable! The avocado, called aguacate in the Spanish speaking world, is indigenous to Mexico and to Central America. It's name in the Nahuatl language was *ahuacatl*, literally meaning "testicle", a reference to it's shape. A member of the *Lauraceae* family, the avocado, *Persea americana*, has many varieties, and new hybrids are constantly being developed as the fruit grows in popularity.

Most avocados are oval or pear-shaped with a large round black seed and a smooth light green pulp. The pulp is soft and buttery when ripe, but to some rather bland. A large smooth green-skinned variety is more typically found in Costa Rica rather than the much darker pebbled skin avocados.

The avocado will not ripen while attached to a tree. It must be picked, utilizing clippers to prevent bruising, then left to sit at room temperature for one to two weeks to ripen. Because of its tannin content, the avocado becomes bitter if cooked. It is primarily eaten raw or added to cooked foods such as soups, stews and omelettes as a last minute garnishment.

Traditionally indians in tropical America have broken open avocados, removed the seed, added salt, and consumed the fruit with tortillas and a beverage, constituting a meal. In North America avocados, which combine well with tomatoes and citrus fruits, are primarily utilized in salads. Their halves are often stuffed with shrimp, crab, or seafood. Mexican mashed avocado, *guacamole*, has gained popularity as a "dip". In our guide we have attempted to include some interesting and out-of-the ordinary recipes utilizing avocados.

Peeled avocados cannot sit for long without turning brown. To prevent flesh discoloration, they can be sprinkled with citrus juice. Should you store a half, keep it unpeeled with the seed embedded, and wrap it in wax paper or plastic--never foil!

The avocado is rich in vitamins and highly digestible, but is too costly to be utilized extensively as a salad oil.

AVOCADO MAYONAISE
Mayonesa de Aguacate

1 large avocado, pittcd and scooped out
2 cloves garlic, crushed
1 T. parsley leaves
2 green onions, including some green,
    trimmed and chopped
1/3 cup vegetable or olive oil
Juice of 1 large lime
1 small jalapeño, seeded (optional)
Salt and pepper

Combine avocado, parsley, garlic cloves, green onions, and jalapeño in a food processor or blender. Pureé. With the machine running, add the oil in a small stream, then the lime juice. Season to taste.

Cover and chill. The mayonaise is good with cold shellfish or a as dip with chips or vegetables.

Makes: 1 1/2 cups.

COLD AVOCADO SOUP
Sopa Fria de Aguacate

2 large ripe avocados, pitted
  and peeled
1/2 cup light cream
1/2 cup non-fat milk
4 cups chilled chicken broth

1 T. butter
2 green onions, minced
1 tsp. fresh ginger, grated
Salt to taste
Chopped chives for garnish

Melt the butter in a pan and sauté the ginger and green onions for about 3 minutes. Cool.

Place the avocado, cream, milk, chicken broth, and lime juice in a blender and blend until smooth. Add the ginger mixture. Put in a container, cover, and refrigerate. Can be made up to one day in advance.

Serve the soup in chilled bowls sprinkled with chives.

Serves: 4 to 6

FIESTA SALAD
Ensalada de Fiesta

Vinaigrette:
1 small garlic clove
1/4 cup fresh cilantro, washed
  and spun dry
3 T. fresh lime juice, or to taste

1/2 tsp. sugar
1/4 tsp. salt
1/2 cup olive oil

Salad:
14 oz. can hearts of palm
4 firm, ripe avocados

1 sm. red onion, thinly sliced
Lettuce leaves (about
  two heads)

In a blender purée the garlic and cilantro with lime juice, sugar, and salt. With the motor running, add the oil in a stream, blending until the dressing is emulsified.

Cut the palmito and avocado into 1/4 inch cubes and in a large bowl with a rubber spatula gently toss with the onion and the vinaigrette until mixed well.

Line eight salad plates with the lettuce leaves and mound the avocado mixture on top.

Serves: 6 to 8

AVOCADO-ORANGE SALAD
Ensalada de Aguacate y Naranja

Salad:
4 medium oranges
2 large ripe avocados

2 green onions, including
   tops, sliced

Cumin Dressing:
5 T. olive oil
1 T. red wine vinegar
1 T. orange juice

1 tsp. sugar
1/4 tsp. ground cumin
1 small clove garlic

Dressing: Whisk together the ingredients in a small bowl. Cover and let stand for at least 1 hour or refrigerate for up to two days.

Peel the oranges and trim away all the white membrane. Cut crosswise into 1/4 inch slices. Pit and peel the avocados. Cut lenghtwise into 1/2 inch wedges.

Arrange the orange and avocado slices on a platter and pour the cumin dressing over them. Sprinkle the green onions over the salad and serve.

Serves: 4

AVOCADO AND SEA BASS CEVICHE
Ceviche de Aguacate y Corvina

2 lbs. sea bass or white fish fillets
1 fresh hot red pepper, julienned
1 small sweet red pepper, julienned
1/2 small purple onion, julienned
2 ripe tomatoes, seeded, chopped,
   and cut into 1/4 inch cubes
1 garlic clove, finely minced
2 tsp. brown sugar

2 T. chopped fresh cilantro
2 T. chopped fresh parsley
salt and pepper to taste
2 cups fresh lime juice
2 avocados, peeled and cut
   into 16 slices, brushed
   with lime juice
chopped parsley (garnish)

Cut the fish fillets into bite-sized pieces. In a large glass bowl, combine all the ingredients except the avocados and the parsley for a garnish. Add the fish and toss gently, but throughly, being certain the fish is well coated with citrus juice.

Cover and refrigereate for at least 5 hours, or until the fish looses its translucent appearance. Stir occasionally during the marination.

Serve in indvidual bowls garnished with avocado slices and additional chopped parsley.

Serves: 8 as a first course

29

"MAMBO" CHICKEN
Pollo Mambo

Chicken:

3/4 cup dry white wine
1/4 cup orange juice
2 T. lime juice
1 T. chopped fresh basil
1 T. vegetable oil

1 T. cracked black peppercorns
1 fresh rosemary sprig or
  1 tsp. dried, crumbled
2 small bay leaves
4 boneless chicken breasts, halved

Salsa:

1 ripe mango, peeled, pitted, diced
3 T. minced onion
3 T. diced green pepper
3 T. diced red bell pepper
1 1/2 T. white wine vinegar

1 T. chopped fresh cilantro
1 T. olive oil
1 tsp. minced fresh chives
1/2 large avocado, peeled,
  pitted, and diced

Mix all the chicken ingredients in a large bowl. Add the chicken and turn to coat. Cover and refrigerate for 4 hours.

Mix all the salsa ingredients, except the avocado, in a large bowl. (This can be done 3 hours ahead. Cover and chill.) Just before serving, add the avocado to the salsa and stir gently to combine. Season with salt and pepper.

Prepare the barbecue grill or use an oven broiler. Remove the chicken from the marinade. Season the chicken with salt and pepper. Grill or broil until cooked through, turning occasionally, about 10 minutes. Transfer the chicken to plates and serve with the salsa.

Serves: 4

BANANA/BANANO

The banana, referred to as *banano* in Spanish, is one of the most important tropical fruits and is consumed world-wide. It is thought to have originated in Malaysia and to have been brought by travelers to tropical Africa. Shortly after the discovery of the Americas, Europeans transported banana plants to this region. The countries of Central American became known as the "Banana Republics" when multinational companies entered the area to cultivate and export the fruit. During the last couple of decades, Central America's cultivation and exportation of bananas has diminished, but the banana still remains a very important commercial product. In Latin America, Costa Rica is second only to Ecuador as a producer/exporter of bananas.

It is a misnomer to call the banana plant a "tree". Bananas grow in"bunches" from a flowering stalk. They are a very economical crop because a single plant can produce hundreds of pounds of fruit and because they are easily harvested.

Actually, "banana" is a general term embracing a number of species or hybrids in the biological family,

Musaceae. The most common bananas found in Costa Rica are the Gros Michel and the Congo along with the "*jardinero*", a midget home grown variety. The latter have more intense flavor than the common yellow banana, thus they are excellent for salads and blender drinks. The "*guineo*" is another small banana available in local markets. It has an excellent flavor, but because it is hard and cannot be eaten raw; it's utilized primarily in soups and stews. It also makes a superb vinegar.

Bananas should be ripened without refrigerating. It's best to buy ones which are firm and plump and a little green, then ripen them in a brown paper bag at room temperature. Only after ripening should bananas be refrigerated. Once opened or refrigerated, bananas will darken unless sprinkled with citrus juice.

The banana, along with a cousin, the plantain (*platano*), is utilized extensively in Central American cooking. The banana can be eaten raw, cooked as a starchy vegetable, dried, and even used fermented to make alcohol. Additionally, the leaves of the banana plant are used in the production of paper and to wrap tamales!

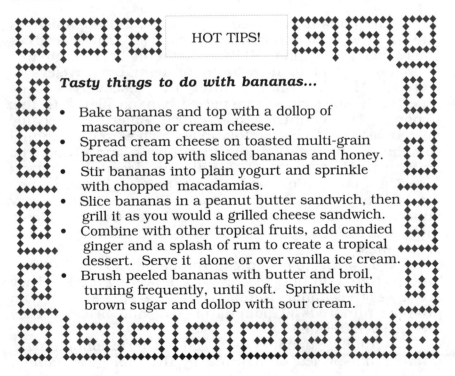

HOT TIPS!

Tasty things to do with bananas...

- Bake bananas and top with a dollop of mascarpone or cream cheese.
- Spread cream cheese on toasted multi-grain bread and top with sliced bananas and honey.
- Stir bananas into plain yogurt and sprinkle with chopped macadamias.
- Slice bananas in a peanut butter sandwich, then grill it as you would a grilled cheese sandwich.
- Combine with other tropical fruits, add candied ginger and a splash of rum to create a tropical dessert. Serve it alone or over vanilla ice cream.
- Brush peeled bananas with butter and broil, turning frequently, until soft. Sprinkle with brown sugar and dollop with sour cream.

BANANA–HEARTS OF PALM SALAD
Ensalada de Banano y Palmito

10 green bananas
1 16 oz. can or jar of palmito
2 hard boiled eggs, chopped
1 cup mayonnaise
1 tablespoon Dijon mustard
1 bunch cilantro, chopped

1 small onion, minced finely
1 bell pepper, minced finely
1 celery rib, minced
1 teaspoon white pepper
2 cubes chicken bouillon

Peel and cook the bananas in water and chicken bouillon. When tender, remove from the water, let cool, and chop finely. Mix the bananas with the onions, cilantro, celery, palmito, and eggs, Blend the mustard, mayonnaise, and white pepper. Add to the banana mixture. Refrigerate and serve on individual plates on top of lettuce leaves.
Serves: 8 to 10

BRAZILIAN CHICKEN BREASTS WITH SAUTEED BANANAS
Pechugas de Pollo Brasileño con Bananos

5 T. butter
2 large firm ripe bananas, peeled
    and sliced lengthwise
2 whole chicken breasts (about 2
    lbs.), skinned, boned, and halved

1 T. vegetable oil
Salt and pepper to taste
1/4 tsp. ground ginger
1/3 cup dry white wine
3 T. dark rum

In a saute pan or heavy skillet over medium heat, melt 3 tablespoons butter. Saute the bananas for 4 to 5 minutes, until brown and crispy. Transfer to a heated platter and set aside.
Add the remaining 2 tablespoons butter and the vegetable oil to the sauté pan; increase the heat to medium-high. Sprinkle the chicken breasts with ginger and salt and pepper. Saute for 3 to 5 minutes on each side. Remove the breasts to a heated platter and keep warm.
Turn the heat to very low. Add the rum to the saute pan, and after it heats through, about 30 seconds, touch a lighted kitchen match to the rum gently and allow the alcohol to burn off, stirring the sauce as the flame subsides. (Be careful to keep your head out of the way, as alcohol flames can shoot up.)
Return the chicken breasts to the pan. Add the white wine and cook over medium heat for 3 minutes, or until the sauce begins to thicken.

33

Put the chicken breasts on the platter between the banana slices, and pour on the sauce.
Serves: 4

BANANA SOUR CREAM PIE
Pie de Banano y Natilla

Crust:

2 1/2 cups crushed graham
  crackers or *Galletas Maria*
6 T. butter, melted with
3 tsp. honey

1/2 teaspoon cinammon
Dash of nutmeg
1/2 cup finely chopped
macadamia nuts

Combine the above ingredients. Mix well, then firmly press into a 9" pie pan, building up the sides. Brown in a 350° oven for 10 minutes. Cool before filling.

Filling:

12 oz. softened cream cheese
1/2 cup sour cream
1/4 cup honey
1 tsp. vanilla extract

1/4 tsp. almond extract
2 mashed ripe bananas
2 T. fresh lemon juice

Beat together all ingredients until well blended. Pour into the cooled crust. Chill at least three hours before serving.
Serves: 8 to 10

CHOCOLATE-BANANA SIN CAKE
Queque Pecado de Chocolate y Banano

Cake:

1 lb. semi-sweet chocolate
8 T. (1 stick) unsalted butter,
  cut into tablespoon size pieces
4 large eggs, separated

4 T. granulated sugar
1 T. cornstarch
2 tsp. vanilla extract
1/4 tsp. cream of tartar

Banana Topping:

1 lb. ripe bananas
2 T. fresh orange juice
3 T. unsalted butter
1 cup heavy whipping cream

3 T. confectioner's sugar
1 T. light rum, or to taste
1 piece (1 ounce) semisweet
  chocolate, for shaving

34

Preheat the oven to 350°F. Butter a 10-inch spring-form pan, and sprinkle with sugar.

Prepare the cake: Cut the chocolate into pieces and melt in the top of a double boiler over simmering water. When the chocolate has completely melted, whisk in the butter, a tablespoon at a time. Let the mixture cool slightly.

Meanwhile, beat the egg yolks with 2 tablespoons of the granulated sugar in a mixer at high speed until the mixture is ivory colored and as thick as marshmallow topping, about 5 minutes. Stir in the cornstarch and vanilla.

Beat the egg whites in a separate bowl, adding the cream of tartar after 20 seconds, then adding the remaining 2 tablespoons of sugar as the whites stiffen to soft peaks. Gently fold the egg yolk mixture into the chocolate mixture; then fold in the egg whites as gently as possible.

Spoon the batter into the prepared pan. Bake the cake until firm on top, but the center is still a little soft, about 30 minutes. Remove the pan from the oven, set on a wire rack, and let the cake cool to room temperature. Run a knife around the inside edge of the pan and remove the sides. The cake will sink a little in the center.

Meanwhile, prepare the topping: Peel the bananas and cut them into 1/4 inch slices. Toss the bananas with the orange juice to prevent discoloring.

Combine the butter and granulated sugar in a large skillet over high heat and cook until the mixture begins to caramelize, 2 to 3 minutes. Stir in the bananas and cook, turning, until golden brown, 3 to 4 minutes. Let the banana mixture cool completely.

Beat the cream in a chilled bowl with a mixer. As the cream stiffens, beat in the confectioners' sugar and rum to taste. Continue beating until stiff.

Spoon the caramelized banana mixture on top of the cake. Using a pastry bag fitted with a star tip, pipe rosettes of the whipped cream all over the top of the cake. Use a vegetable peeler or paring knife to shave the chocolate over the cake. Cut into wedges for serving.

Serves: 8 to 10

CASHEW/MARANON

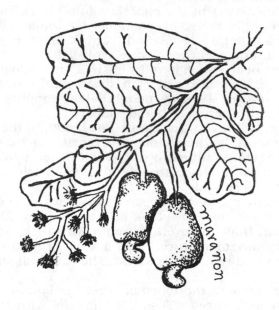

The marañon, *anacardium occidentale*, is known by most of the world as the cashew   The evergreen cashew tree has both a fruit, the cashew apple, and the nut, *semilla de marañon* in Spanish.   The kidney-shaped nut grows as an appendage to the pear-shaped fruit.   Between the outside shell and the nut is a very irritating toxic oil--the cashew is related to poison ivy and poison sumac! Thus, the nut must be handled with gloves and dried (roasted) before being eaten. In rural areas of Costa Rica this is accomplished over an open fire.

The cashew tree is indigenous to the West Indies, Central America, Peru, and Brazil.   The nut is the tree's biggest gift! After roasting, there is high export demand for cashews as a upscale snack food. Cashew nuts have a sweet, buttery flavor, but beware--they are about 48% fat!

The cashew apple has frequently been overlooked. Its flesh is tart and astringent, thus it is not favored for out-of-hand eating, but it can be used to make wine, syrup, and vinegar or it can be candied or made into jam or chutney.

A popular beverage amongst rural Costa Ricans is *fruta de marañon* made by liquefying the pulp of the cashew apple in a blender and adding sugar and water. Campesinos will swear cashew juice is a cure for dysentery!!

Marañon fruits are often hard to find in San José, but are found in towns along both coasts. The dried fruit is available in Central Valley public markets and looks like a cross between a prune and a fig. Orotina is reputed to be the cashew capital of Costa Rica.

CASHEW DIPPING SAUCE
Salsa de Semilla de Marañon

1 cup unsalted roasted cashews
   (about 1/4 lb.)
2 cloves, garlic, minced
1 T. fresh lime juice, or to taste
1 T. vegetable oil
3/4 cup plain yogurt
1 T. soy sauce, or to taste
cayenne to taste

In a food processor blend the cashews with the oil, scraping down the sides, until the mixture forms a paste. Add remaining ingredients, salt and pepper to taste, and blend until smooth.

The dipping sauce may be made up to 4 days ahead and kept chilled, covered. Return the sauce to room temperature before serving.

Can be used as a dipping sauce for shrimp, chicken nuggets, egg rolls, and raw vegetables such as snow peas, scallions, carrot and sweet pepper slices, etc.

Makes: About 1 1/2 cups

LEAFY CASHEW SALAD
Ensalada con Lechuga y Maránon

1 1/2 tsp. white-wine vinegar
2 tsp. Dijon-style mustard
2 T. olive oil
2 T. roasted cashews, chopped fine

4 cups torn red-leaf lettuce,
   rinsed and spun dry
2 cups torn endive (chicory),
   rinsed and spun dry

In a bowl whisk together the vinegar and mustard. Salt and pepper to taste and whisk in the oil. Whisk until the dressing is emulsified.

Add the red-leaf lettuce, the endive, and the cashews. Toss well.

Serves: 2

GREEN BEANS WITH CASHEWS
Vainicas con Semillas de Marañon

1 1/2 lbs. green beans
3 T. sweet butter, melted
1 cup cashews

1/2 tsp. black pepper
3/4 tsp. salt
1/4 cup chopped parsley

Blanch the green beans in boiling salted water.

While beans are cooking, melt the butter and add salt, pepper and parsley. Stir to mix.

Drain beans and place in a warm bowl. Sprinkle cashews on top and then pour butter mixture over the beans. Toss well. Arrange in a serving dish and serve immediately.

Serves: 6

BEEF TENDERLOIN WITH CASHEWS
Lomito con Semillas de Marañon

1 beef tenderloin, about 3 lbs.
   or 1 1/2 kilos
8 oz. cashew nuts
3 garlic cloves, crushed, but
   unpeeled

4 oz. butter or 1/2 butter
   and 1/2 vegetable oil
2 sprigs fresh thyme
2 sprigs fresh oregano
Salt and pepper to taste

Sauce:
4 red sweet peppers
1 1/2 cups beef broth
4 T. butter

1/2 cup sour cream
4 T. brandy

The evening before, marinate the beef tenderloin with the garlic and salt and pepper.

The following day, brown all sides of the beef in butter along with the thyme, oregano, garlic cloves, and cashews. Remove the cashews when they are golden. Continue to cook the beef until desired degree of doneness. Remove from the stove top and keep warm in the oven while preparing the sauce.

Chop the red peppers and cook them in the beef broth. When soft, remove and cool, then puree in the blender. Pour the puree into the pan used to brown the beef. Add butter in pieces, sour cream and brandy, simmering at a low heat to make sure the mixture does not boil. Add the beef tenderloin and the cashews just before serving. Slice and serve.

Serves: 12

COCONUT/COCO

Coco

The coconut, *coco*, is the most economically important member of the palm family, *Palmae*. Since the tree grows in tropical lowlands and its fruits are distributed by ocean currents, the coconut is most typically found in the coastal regions of Central America. It supplies drink and is utilized heavily in cooking, particularly on the Atlantic coast of Central America. Historically, the shell has provided domestic utensils and fiber. The fronds can furnish the raw materials for hats, mats, baskets, and thatch. The wood can be used as timber. The blossoms produce a sap which can be fermented into an alcoholic beverage.

Here in Costa Rica there are several types of coco trees. Some can grow as tall as one hundred feet and may live as long as one hundred years. The Caribbean type is a lofty giant while the Pacific area has the dwarf or "*enano*" varieties. The latter produce more rapidly and are preferred for "*pipas*", whole coconut drinks served directly out of the shell.

The most important part of the coco tree is the nut. It's the world's largest seed, and it's "meat" and "milk" (best described as "water") are utilized heavily in Caribbean style cooking. If you have interest in the water, pierce the three "eyes" with an ice pick or screwdriver, and drain it out. Drink the liquid, if you desire, but do not confuse it with "coconut milk". We provide below a recipe for making coconut milk.

It's difficult to extract the "meat" from a coconut. It must be obtained by using a machete or a hammer or by slamming the nut against a very hard surface. Better yet, raw "meat" can be found at downtown fruit stands.

It's best to buy coconuts which feel heavy for their size. Shake them to be sure you can hear the water sloshing inside and check the "eyes" to make sure they are not wet or moldy.

Coconut "meat" and "milk" are used worldwide in the preparation of sauces, curries, and desserts. The milk is an exquisite flavoring in rice dishes. Coconut cream makes wonderful puddings, ice creams, and cakes, as well as luscious tropical drinks like *Piña Coladas*. Coconut oil, originally utilized in soap manufacture, has become an important source of vegetable oil and the basis for margarine.

COCONUT MILK
Leche de Coco

Freshly grated flesh of a mature coconut
3 cups boiling water

Coconut milk isn't the clear liquid in the center of a coconut--that's coconut water! Coconut milk is a creamy extract made in the following manner...

Combine the grated coconut and the boiling water in a blender or food processor and puree for 2 minutes. Let this mixture stand for 15 minutes.

Strain the mixture through a strainer lined with several layers of dampened cheese cloth. Twist the cheesecloth tightly to extract as much milk as possible. (The process can be repeated using another 3 cups of boiling water to make a second, thinner batch of coconut milk.) Store the coconut milk in the refrigerator where it will keep for 3 to 4 days. It can also be frozen.

Makes: 3 cups

CARIBBEAN COCONUT CHICKEN
Pollo Caribeño con Coco

2 whole chicken breasts (about 2 lbs.), skinned, boned, halved, and flattened to 1/4 inch thick.

4 thin slices prosciutto or ham
1 ripe mango, peeled and cut into
   8 strips 1-inch wide
1 cup all-purpose flour
1/2 tsp. salt
1/8 tsp. black pepper
1/2 tsp. curry powder
1/8 tsp. finely crumbled dried thyme

2 eggs, well beaten
2 cups grated fresh coconut
   (or unsweetened shredded)
vegetable oil for deep frying
   (2 cups or more)
Juice of 1 fresh lime
1 to 2 limes, cut into wedges

Inside the edge of each pounded chicken breast, place a slice of prosciutto trimmed to 1/2 inch. Place a slice of mango in the center. Roll lengthwise to completely enclose the mango and prosciutto. Tuck in and pinch the ends of the chicken breasts to seal tightly. Arrange the rolls on a baking sheet and refrigerate for about 30 minutes, or until very firm.

In a bowl, combine the flour, salt, pepper, curry powder, and thyme. Spread the mixture on a plate. Pour the beaten eggs into a bowl. Loosely sprinkle the coconut onto another plate.

When the chicken rolls are very cold and firm, roll each in the flour mixture and shake off the excess. Then roll in the beaten eggs until completely covered; drain. Finally, roll in the coconut.

Arrange the chicken rolls on a plate in a single layer. Cover and refrigerate for 30 minutes.

Preheat the oven to 325°F. Heat the oil in a deep heavy skillet. The oil should be deep enough to cover the chicken rolls completely. When the oil is hot enough to deep fry, add half the chicken rolls to the skillet and deep fry until golden brown, or about 4 minutes. Remove with a slotted spoon and drain on several layers of paper towel. Repeat with the remaining chicken rolls.

Put the chicken rolls on a baking sheet and bake for about 10 minutes. Splash with lime juice and serve with lime wedges. In addition to being served as a main course, the rolls can be sliced and served as finger food.

Serves: 4

COCONUT RICE
Arroz con Coco

2 T. cooking oil or butter
2 cloves garlic, minced
2 tsp. minced fresh ginger
1 1/2 cups long grain white rice

1 cup coconut milk
  (See recipe p. 41)
1 1/2 cups water
Salt

Heat the oil in a heavy saucepan over a medium heat. Add the garlic and ginger and cook until fragrant but not brown, about 1 minute. Add the rice and saute until the individual grains are shiny, about 1 minute.

Add the coconut milk, water, and salt and bring to a boil. Reduce the heat, cover the pan, and cook the rice until all the liquid is absorbed and the grains are tender, 18 to 20 minutes. Remove the pan from the heat and let the rice stand for 1 minute and serve at once.

Makes: 3 cups, serving 4

CARIBBEAN FISH STEW
Rondon Caribeño

1/4 cup cooking oil
1 lb. tiquisque
1 lb. ñampi
1 lb. yuca
2 ripe plantains
3 garlic cloves

1 1/2 to 2 llbs. white fish
3 T. parsley, minced
1 cup celery, diced
4 mature coconuts
Salt and pepper to taste

Peel and cut into chunks the tiquisque, ñampi, and yucca. Slice the plantains into 2" thick pieces. Cube the fish. Put all aside.

Open the coconut and save the water. Remove the coconut meat from the shells. Split it into two portions and grind each in a blender. Add 5 cups of boiling water to the coconut meat, strain, and save.

In a large pot, heat the cooking oil. Add the garlic and the other vegetables and saute. Add the coconut water you saved and the milk to make about 6 cups. When the vegetables are fork tender, add the cubed fish and condiments. Cook for another 10 minutes. Serve in a bowl with lime slices on the side.

This is a meal in itself...serve the soup with bread or tortillas.

Serves: 6

COCONUT SOUFFLE
Souffle de Coco

1 1/2 T. unsalted butter, melted	1 cup canned coconut cream
1 cup toasted coconut	6 egg whites
4 egg yolks	1/2 tsp. cream of tartar
4 T. sugar	2 T. all-purpose flour

Tangerine Chocolate Sauce (recipe follows)

Preheat the oven to 400°F. Brush the inside of a 5-cup souffle dish with half of the melted butter, taking special care to coat the inside rim. Place the dish in the freezer for 5 minutes. Brush the souffle dish with the remaining melted butter. (This double buttering prevents the souffle from sticking as it rises.) Sprinkle the inside of the dish with 1/2 cup of the toasted coconut.

Place the egg yolks in a medium-size bowl and whisk in 2 T. of the sugar and flour. Scald the coconut cream in a medium-size heavy saucepan over a high heat.

Whisk the scalded coconut cream into the yolk mixture in a thin stream. Return the yolk mixture to the pan, set over medium heat, and bring the mixture to a boil, whisking steadily. Cook the mixture until bubbly and thickened, about 2 minutes. Remove the pan from the heat and keep hot.

Starting the mixer on low, beat the egg whites, adding the cream of tartar after 20 seconds. Gradually increase the speed to medium, then to high. Sprinkle in the remaining 2 T. sugar as the whites start to stiffen. Continue beating until the whites are firm and glossy, but not dry.

Whisk one-quarter of the whites into the hot yolk mixture to lighten it. Gently fold this mixture back into the remaining whites with a rubber spatula.

Gently spoon one-third of the souffle mixture into the prepared souffle dish. Sprinkle 1/3 cup of the toasted coconut on top. Spoon half of the remaining souffle mixture into the dish and sprinkle with the remaining coconut. Spoon in the remaining souffle mixture. (Any extra can be baked in buttered ramekins.) Smooth the top of the souffle with a wet spatula. Wipe off the outside of the souffle dish with a wet cloth. Run the tip of a paring knife around the inside edge of the dish to clear a path for the rising souffle.

Bake the souffle until puffed and golden brown, 15 to 20 minutes. Don't open the oven door during the first 10 minutes. When you open the door, do so just a crack and close it as quickly and gently as possible. To test for doneness, gently poke the dish with a wooded spoon. The souffle should jiggle just slightly.

Serve the souffle immediately, with Tangerine Chocolate Sauce on the side.
Serves: 4

Tangerine Chocolate Sauce
1/3 cup heavy (or whipping) cream
4 oz. semisweet chocolate, finely chopped
1 to 2 T. tangerine liqueur (You can use Salicsa's *Licor de Naranja*)

Scald the cream in a small heavy saucepan over medium heat. Whisk in the chocolate and cook over low heat until completely melted, about 3 minutes. Whisk in the liqueur, to taste. Serve warm. Any leftover sauce can be stored, covered, in the refrigerator. Reheat the sauce in a double boiler before using.

SHRIMP CURRY
Curry de Camarones

1/2 cup olive oil
1 lb. medium shrimp, peeled
   and deveined
2 medium onions, chopped
3 garlic cloves, finely chopped
2 T. grated fresh ginger
2 tsp. curry powder
1/2 tsp. ground turmeric

2 large ripe tomatoes, peeled
   seeded, and chopped
1 tsp. tomato paste
2 1/2 cups fish or chicken
   stock
1/2 cup fresh coconut milk
   or use sweetened canned
   coconut milk

In a large nonreactive saute pan, heat half the olive oil over a medium heat. Add the shrimp and saute for about 2 minutes or until pink. Remove the shrimp with a slotted spoon and reserve.

Add the onions and a little more of the oil and cook until the onions are translucent. Add the garlic, ginger, curry powder, and turmeric; mix thoroughly and cook for about 3 minutes.

Stir in the tomatoes, tomato paste, stock, and coconut milk, and bring to a boil. Add salt to taste, reduce the heat and simmer for 30 minutes. Add the shrimp and cook for 2 minutes, or until the shrimp are just heated through.

Serve with white rice accompanied by *maduros*. (See our recipe for *maduros*.)
Serves: 4

COCONUT BROWNIES
Brownies de Coco

2 oz. semisweet chocolate
2 oz. unsweetened chocolate
3/4 cup canned coconut cream
1 1/2 cups sugar
3 large eggs, beaten
2 tsp. vanilla extract

1 T. dark rum
1 cup sifted all-purpose flour
1/2 tsp. ground cinnamon
1/8 tsp. ground cloves
1 tsp. baking powder

Preheat the oven to 350°F. Generously butter an 8-inch square cake pan. Melt the chocolates in the coconut cream in the top of a double boiler over simmering water.

Combine the sugar, eggs, vanilla, and rum in a large mixing bowl and whisk until smooth. Whisk in the chocolate mixture. Sift the flour into the mixture, along with the spices and baking powder and whisk just to mix. Pour the batter into the prepared pan.

Bake the brownies until the top is crusty, but the center remains a little soft, about 35 minutes. Let cool completely in the pan on a wire rack. Cut the brownies into 8 rectangles.

Serves: 8

COCONUT CANDY
Cajeta de Coco

14 oz. can condensed milk
1 stick margarine
1 cup brown sugar

2 cups powdered milk
2 cups grated dry coconut
1/2 cup macadamia nuts,
  chopped

In a sauce pan, melt the margarine and add the condensed milk, stirring constantly. Add the brown sugar. When the sugar dissolves, remove the pan from the burner. Add the powdered milk, a little at a time, stirring constantly. When the mixture starts to look dry, add the macadamia nuts and the grated coconut. Form 1 inch balls and let cool.

Makes: 30 to 36 balls.

GUAVA/GUAYABA

Guayaba

Known as guava in North America and Europe, the guayaba, *psidium guajava*, is native to tropical America and the West Indies. Ripe guavas vary in size and color. Their size can be from that of a walnut to the size of a small apple. Their skins vary in color from white, yellow, and green to dark red. All guavas have hard seeds in their sweet-acid pink or white pulp. Guavas with pink pulp, *psidium cattleianum*, have gained the name Strawberry Guava not only for the color of the pulp, but because the flesh has a strawberry-like flavor. There is a Costa Rican tart guava, known locally as *Cas*, which is frequently used in the preparation of natural drinks.

The guava fruit is eaten raw in salads and desserts, but can have a strong sweet, musky odor, so it is usually cooked and utilized in jams, butter, marmalade, chutney, sauces, pies and cakes. It is used as an ice cream flavoring and in tropical fruit drinks. Guavas can be found canned and processed both as a paste or in slices.

47

Ripe guavas bruise easily and are highly perishable, thus the fruit is usually picked under-ripe for export. The flavor is best when guavas are picked ripe. A slight give when pressed indicates a mature fruit.

HOT TIPS!

Try these savory ways of utilizing guavas...

- Spread guava jelly on cream cheese atop nutty brown bread.
- As a cracker spread, top a block of cream cheese with tart guava jelly.
- Swirl pureed guava into yogurt.
- Serve fresh slices with sugar and cream.

BABY BACK RIBS WITH GUAVA BARBECUE SAUCE
Costillas con Salsa Barbacoa de Guayaba

3 lbs. baby back ribs
1 onion, quartered
2 cloves garlic

2 bay leaves
1 tsp. ground cumin

Guava barbecue sauce:
1 cup guava paste
6 T. cider vinegar
1/4 cup dark rum
1/4 cup tomato paste
1/4 cup fresh lime juice
1 T. soy sauce
2 tsp. ketchup
2 tsp. Worcestershire sauce

1 T. minced fresh ginger
2 T. minced fresh onion
2 cloves garlic, minced
1/4 to 1/2 scotch bonnet
    pepper or other hot chili,
    seeded and minced
Salt and pepper to taste

Roasting:
1 onion, thinly sliced
1 tsp. vegetable oil

3 T. fresh lime juice
Salt and pepper to taste

In a large pot, combine the ribs with the onion, garlic, bay leaves, and cumin. Add water to cover and bring to a boil over a high heat. Boil for 5 minutes. Drain the ribs and rinse well.

Meanwhile, combine all the ingredients for the barbecue sauce in a nonreactive heavy saucepan. Simmer until the sauce is slightly thickened and richly flavored, about 5 minutes. Correct the seasonings, adding salt or pepper to taste.

Preheat the oven to 250°F. Place the sliced onion in the bottom of a nonreactive roasting pan. Add water to a depth of 1 inch. Place a roasting rack on top and brush the rack with the oil. Sprinkle the ribs with lime juice, and salt and pepper, and brush on both sides with half of the barbecue sauce. Tightly tent the pan with aluminum foil. Bake the ribs until very tender, about 2 hours. (The recipe can be prepared several hours ahead to this stage.)

Preheat a barbecue grill to very hot or preheat the broiler with the tray 3 inches from the heat. Just before serving, grill or broil the ribs until crusty and brown, 2 to 3 minutes per side, brushing with the remaining guava barbecue sauce.

Serves: 4 to 6

GUAVA CHEESECAKE
Cheesecake de Guayaba

Crust:
1 1/4 cups chocolate cookie crumbs or graham cracker crumbs
1/3 cup melted butter   2 T. sugar

Filling:
1 cup guava paste   2 cups sugar, or to taste
1/2 cup fresh lemon juice   4 extra large eggs
2 lbs. cream cheese at room   2 T. vanilla extract
   temperature   1 T. grated lemon zest

Glaze:

1/4 cup red currant jelly   About 1 T. water

49

Preheat the oven to 350°F. Butter a 9-inch spring form pan. Prepare the crust. Mix together the cookie crumbs, melted butter, and sugar in a mixing bowl to form a crumbly dough. Press the dough over the bottom and up the sides of the spring form pan. Bake the crust until almost dry, about 10 minutes. Set aside to cool. Leave the oven on.

Meanwhile, prepare the filling: Melt the guava paste in the lemon juice in a nonreactive heavy saucepan, whisking steadily, over medium heat, 2 to 3 minutes. Let the mixture cool slightly.

Beat the cream cheese in a large bowl with a mixer. Add the sugar and beat until light and fluffy. Beat in the eggs, one at a time, beating until each is incorporated before adding the next, and scraping down the sides of the bowl frequently. Beat in the vanilla, lemon zest, and melted guava paste. Correct the flavorings, adding sugar to suit your taste. Pour the filling into the prepared pan.

Bring 1 quart of water to a boil. Wrap a sheet of aluminum foil around the bottom and sides of the spring form pan to prevent water from seeping in. Place the pan in a large roasting pan and pour in 1 inch of boiling water.

Bake the cheesecake until the top is firm and the filling no longer jiggles when the pan is shaken, about 1 1/4 or 1 1/2 hours. If the top of the cheesecake starts to brown before the filling sets, tent the cake with aluminum foil. When the cake is done, turn off the heat, open the oven door a few inches, and let the cheesecake cool for 20 minutes. Transfer the cheesecake to a wire rack to cool completely. Cover and refrigerate for at least 6 hours, preferably overnight.

Prepare the glaze: Melt the red currant jelly in the water in a small saucepan, whisking steadily, over medium heat, until the mixture is the consistency of heavy cream. Thin with additional water, if necessary. Gently brush the top of the cheesecake with the glaze. Cover and chill for at least 30 minutes. To serve, run a slender knife around the sides of the spring form pan. Remove the sides and serve.

Serves: 10

LIME/LIMON

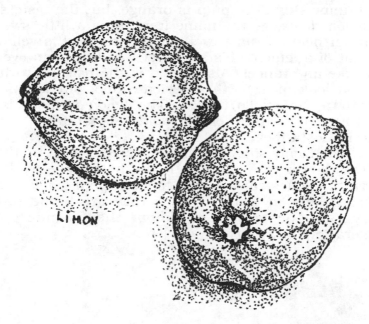

LIMON

Limón is the Spanish name for both the lemon and the lime; however, lemons as we know them in North America are almost nonexistent in Central America. The lime is the "lemon" of the topics! The lime, *Citrus aurantifolia*, is found on an evergreen tree of the *Rutaceae* family. Although very tangy and higher in acidity, a lime can be substituted for the lemon in most recipes.

The lime is thought to have originated in the Indo-Malayan region and to have been brought to Europe by Crusaders who found it in North Africa and the Middle East. (In Arabic the fruit is called límah.) The Spanish are responsible for this citrus fruit's appearance in the New World. For centuries, British sailors consumed lime juice as a preventive against scurvy, hence the origin of the slang name "limey" to refer to the British!

Many varieties of the lime are found in Costa Rica. The Mexican lime, called *limón criollo* or *limón acido,* is the most popular locally. It is small, sometimes no larger than a ping-pong ball, with a thin, smooth deep-green skin. It has more juice than some varieties, so the *criollo/acido* is especially suited for drinks and to squeeze over fish, avocados, and the like. The *limón*

51

mandarina can also be found. It looks like a tangerine with bumpy skin. The pulp is orange, but the taste sour. The *limón dulce*, as the name implies, is a little sweeter, but nevertheless a lime even though its peel is yellowish like that of a lemon. It's so sweet the *dulce* can even be eaten like an orange! Also found is the *bencino* with the size and look of a North American lime, but it has less juice than the *criollo/acido*. The *limón mesina*, larger and rougher than a *criollo/acido*, is another variety found in Costa Rica.

When choosing limes, the general rule of thumb is, "The darker green the peel, the higher the acidity of the fruit". Limes can be kept fresh in your home for 2-3 weeks, if kept in water. Since they are prone to cold injury, its best not to keep them under high refrigeration.

CREAMY LIME DRESSING
Aderezo de Limón

5 T. fresh lime juice
1 cup light olive oil
2 eggs
Grated zest of 2 limes
2 T. Dijon mustard
Fresh ground pepper, to taste
1 cup corn oil

Place the lime juice, eggs, and mustard in the bowl of a food processor or in a blender, and process for 15 seconds. With the motor running, slowly pour in the oils until the mayonnaise has thickened. Transfer the mixture to a bowl, and fold in the lime zest and pepper. Cover and refrigerate until ready to use.

This creamy dressing is great drizzled over salads with sliced avocados, oranges, or tomatoes as well as chicken salad with green grapes.

Makes: 2 3/4 cups

LIME FISH MARINADE
Marinada de Limón para Pescado

Juice of 3 limes   1/2 cup olive oil
3/4 cup chopped cilantro

Mix the ingredients and add to fish. Makes enough marinade for 3 lbs. fish. After marinading your fish, either grill or bake it.
Makes: 3/4 cup

LIME AND TORTILLA SOUP
Sopa de Limones y Tortillas

2 corn tortillas   4 cups chicken broth
oil for frying   1 cup cooked chicken,
2 tsp. vegetable oil   shredded
1/3 cup onion, chopped   1 tomato, chopped
1 bell pepper, peeled, roasted,   1 T. lime juice
   and chopped *or*   4 large lime slices
1/4 cup canned chopped green chiles

Cut the tortillas into 2" x 1/2" strips, then fry the strips in hot oil until brown and crisp. Drain on paper towels.

Heat two teaspoons of vegetable oil in a large sauce pan. Add the onions and chile. Saute until tender. Add the broth and chicken and salt to taste. Cover and simmer for 20 minutes. Add the chopped tomato and simmer 5 minutes longer. Stir in the lime juice, taste, and add more if desired.

Pour into serving bowls and add the tortilla strips. Float a lime slice in the center of each bowl.
Serves: 4

LIME SORBET
Sorbet de Limón

2 1/2 cups fresh lime juice   1 1/3 cups sugar
   (10-12 large limes)   1 cup light rum
Zest of 3 limes   1/2 cup water

Process all the ingredients in a blender. Freeze in an ice cream maker or small cups. It can also be frozen and served in a half lime, with all its pulp removed.
Makes: 1 quart

LIME AND MACADAMIA TART
Torta de Limón y Macadamia

Pastry:

1 1/2 cups flour
1/2 cup cold butter, cut into
   small pieces
1 to 2 T. ice water

1 T. sugar
Pinch of salt
1 egg yolk

Filling:

2 large limes
1/2 cup unsalted macadamias,
   ground

1/2 cup sugar
2 eggs
6 T. melted butter

To make the pastry, process the flour, butter, sugar, and salt in a food processor fitted with a steel blade until the mixture resembles coarse meal. Add the egg yolk. With the machine running, add enough water for the dough to gather into a ball. Remove the dough, dust with flour, wrap in plastic wrap, and refrigerate for an hour.

Preheat the oven to 400°F. Roll out the dough into a 12 inch circle. Line a 9 inch tart pan with a removable bottom. Using a fork, prick small openings all over the bottom of the dough. Line the dough with wax paper and weight with dry beans so the dough adheres tightly to the pan. Bake the shell for 15 minutes, then remove the weights and let the shell cool.

To prepare the lime zest, remove the peel carefully with a vegetable peeler, then chop it fine with a chef's knife. Place the zest, sugar, eggs, and ground macadamias in a food processor fitted with a steel blade, and blend for about 20 seconds. Squeeze the juice from the lime and add the butter to the mixture. Process 10 seconds more.

Pour the filling into the shell and bake for 30 minutes at 400°F, or until firm and golden. To serve, top with whipped cream and garnish with a macadamia.

Serves: 6 to 8

LYCHEE/MAMON CHINO

The mamón chino, *Litchi chinensis*, is the most renowned of a group of edible fruits of the soapberry family, *Sapindaceae*. The English name lychee "nut" is erroneous as it is the fruit rather than the nut which is eaten. The lychee is native to China and was brought to Europe in the 19th century by way of Burma and India.

The lychee tree produces clusters of an oval fruit about an inch in diameter. The fruit has a rough red knobby skin, but after drying the skin turns to a light brown. A gelatinous white flesh with a sweet-tart taste surrounds a single shiny brown seed. The flavor of the lychee hints at honey and muscat grapes. To open the lychee, cut it in half around the middle, down to the seed. Twist the halves in opposite directions to free one half. Pluck the seed from the remaining half with your fingers, then suck out the raw flesh. Or you can pinch the skin at the rounded part of each half to pop out the fruit.

The fruit Costa Ricans call mamón chino, however, is not a true lychee, but a fruit closely related to the lychee, the rambutan. The rambutan tastes like a lychee, but is usually a little larger with a more brittle shell. Its most distinctive feature is the shell's long soft red spines. The fruit attracts much interest from visitors to Costa Rica when they first view it at a number of fruit stands in downtown San José.

Picked lychees and rambutans perish quickly. At room temperature they keep their color and quality for only about 3-5 days. For this reason, they are sometimes dried because they can be stored up to a year without a change in texture or flavor. A few days after picking, the fruit naturally dehydrates and the flesh becomes dry and shriveled like a raisin. Peeled and seeded lychees are canned in sugar and syrup for export. They usually can be found amongst the Oriental food products in supermarkets.

Aside from eating lychees or rambutans fresh, the fruit, when peeled and pitted, can be added to fruit cups and fruit salads. Dried lychees may be stuffed with cream cheese or pecan meats to make appetizers. Pureed lychees can be added to ice cream. Lychees may be spiced or pickled or made into preserves or wine.

LYCHEE SAUCE
Salsa de Mamón Chino

1 lb. fresh lychees, halved, seeded, and peeled (2 cups flesh)
1/2 yellow bell pepper, cored, seeded, and diced
1/2 red bell pepper, cored, seeded, and diced
Salt and fresh ground pepper to taste

3 scallions, trimmed & finely chopped
3 to 4 T. fresh lime juice
1 T. finely chopped candied ginger
1 T. honey (optional)

Combine all of the ingredients in a mixing bowl, and gently toss to mix. Correct the seasonings, adding salt, lime juice, or honey to taste. The sauce should be a little sweet and a little sour. Serve it with poultry. It goes exceptionally well with duck.
Makes: 2 cups

LYCHEE CHICKEN WITH SWEET/SOUR SAUCE
Pollo con Mamón Chino en Salsa Agri-dulce

1 lb. skinless chicken fillets,
  cut into 1 inch pieces
1 tsp. salt

6 T. cornstarch
1 egg
2 cups oil for deep frying

Sauce:
6 T. catsup
6 T. white vinegar
6 T. sugar
1/2 onion cubed
1/2 red pepper cubed

20 lychees
3 T. cornstarch, dissolved in
  3 T. water
1 1/2 cups cold water

Combine the salt, egg, and cornstarch. Mix well and add the chicken fillet pieces.

In a pan suitable for deep frying, heat the oil until smoking hot. Drop the chicken pieces into the oil, one at a time. Deep fry until crisp, about 3 to 5 minutes. Remove the chicken and set aside. Save the oil.

In a sauce pan, put the catsup, vinegar, sugar, and water. Bring to a boil. Reduce the heat, and stir in the cornstarch mixture. Add the onions, peppers, and lychees, and heat until cooked.

Place the chicken pieces on a platter and pour the sauce over the top. Serve with white rice.

Serves: 4 to 6

LYCHEES IN CUSTARD SAUCE
Mamón Chino con Crema Pastelera

15 to 20 lychees, peeled and
  seeded or equivalent canned
1 1/2 cups unsweetened
  evaporated milk

5 T. sugar
1 tsp. vanilla
5 eggs at room temperature,
  separated

Separate the egg yolks from the whites. Whisk the egg whites until soft peaks form. Place in vegetable steamer (or a sieve or fine colander over a pan) and steam until firm. Set aside.

In a sauce pan, beat the egg yolks and add the sugar and evaporated milk.   Stir over a low heat until the mixture becomes a smooth custard, then remove it from the heat, add vanilla, and cool.

Place the lychees in a serving bowl and pour the cool custard over them. Spoon the egg whites on top. Refrigerate before serving.

Serves: 4 to 6

MACADAMIA

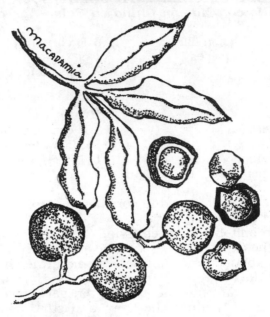

The macadamia nut is familiar to most North Americans and Europeans. It comes from two species of evergreen subtropical Australian trees and is sometimes called the "Queensland nut" because of its Australian origin. The first commercial macadamia orchards were planted in Hawaii in the 1922's. Prized for its texture and flavor, the growing popularity of the nut has lead to the establishment of plantations in Costa Rica during the last decade. However, macadamias are primarily an export crop and are not utilized much in Central American cooking.

The macadamia is a handsome tree with evergreen holly-like leaves. Clusters of blossoms can produce up to 100 pounds of the fruit 8-10 years after planting. The edible portion is enclosed in a hard brown shell that, in turn, is encased in a leathery husk. When the seed matures, the husk splits open, and the nut falls out. In the drying process, heat cures the nut and shrinks it away from its shell. Macadamia meat should be white. Yellowing indicates the oil in the nut has become rancid.

In Asia the macadamia is used in stews and other dishes, but in Europe and North America it is principally an upscale cocktail snack. However, macadamias are growing in use both in cooking and as garnishments for salads and entrees. They are a great coating for fish fillets and chicken breasts. They are also delicious in baked goods and can be substituted for walnuts and pecans which ,when available, are expensive in Costa Rica.

MACADAMIA CRUSTED SEA BASS
Corvina con Macadamia

1 1/2 lbs. corvina fillets
2 eggs beaten
3 T. clarified butter* OR 1 1/2 T. butter
     & 1 1/2 T. olive oil or cooking oil
1 cup lightly salted macadamias
1 cup fine, dried bread crumbs
1 cup all-purpose flour
Salt and Pepper to taste
Lime wedges, for serving

To clarify butter: Melt unsalted butter in a saucepan over a low heat. Skim off any white foam which rises to the surface. Then carefully pour off the clear yellow liquid (the clarified butter), leaving the milky residue.

Rinse the fish fillets and pat dry. Season the fillets on both sides with salt and pepper. Grind the macadamia nuts and bread crumbs to a fine powder in a food processor, running the machine in short bursts. Do not over grind or the mixture will become oily. Place the nut mixture in a shallow bowl, the flour in another, and the eggs in a third.

Just before serving, melt the butter in a large non-stick frying pan over a medium heat. Dip each piece of fish first in flour, shaking off the excess, then in the beaten egg, and finally in the macadamia nut mixture. Pan-fry the fish until crusty and golden brown, about 2 minutes per side. Blot the fish on paper towels and transfer to plates or a platter for serving. Garnish with the lime wedges.

Serves: 4

MACADAMIA-COCONUT PIE
Pie de Macadamia y Coco

1 1/2 cups milk	4 eggs
1 cup granulated sugar	1 1/2 tsp. vanilla extract
1 cup shredded coconut	3/4 tsp. baking powder
1/2 cup all purpose flour	1/4 tsp. salt
1/4 cup chopped macadamias, roasted	1/2 stick butter, room temp.
	whipping cream

Topping:
Toasted shredded coconut and chopped macadamias

Preheat the oven to 325°F. Grease a 10 inch pie pan. Blend all the ingredients in a blender or a food processor until well mixed. Pour into the greased pan. Bake until golden brown and firm to touch, about 35 minutes. Sprinkle the toasted coconut and macadamias over the top. Serve warm, passing the cream separately.

Serves: 6 to 8

MILK CANDY WITH MACADAMIAS
Cajeta con Macadamia

1 4 oz. can of evaporated milk	1 tsp. ground cinnamon
1 1/2 to 2 cups sugar	1/2 cup of chopped and
1 T. butter	toasted macadamias

In a heavy sauce pan boil the milk with all the ingredients except the nuts, stirring constantly with a wooden spoon until very thick, about 50 minutes, or until the bottom of the sauce pan can been seen clearly. Be careful not to burn the mixture.

Remove the sauce pan from the burner and add the nuts. Pour the mixture into a greased 8-inch square pyrex dish and let harden.

Makes: 16 squares

MACADAMIA-COCONUT BISCOTTI
Biscotti de Macadamia y Coco

1 stick of butter, room temperature 2 1/4 cups of flour
3/4 cup firmly packed brown sugar 1 1/2 tsp. baking powder
2 large eggs   1/4 tsp. salt
1/2 cup and 2 T. shredded coconut 1 cup chopped macadamias,
                                              roasted

Cream the butter and sugar in a mixing bowl. Add the eggs, one at a time, beating well after each addition. Beat in the shredded coconut.

Mix the flour, baking powder, and salt in a medium-sized bowl. Gradually stir the dry ingredients into the butter and sugar mixture. Mix in the macadamias. Cover and refrigerate the dough for 30 minutes.

Preheat the oven to 350°F. Line a cookie sheet with wax paper. Divide the dough in half, and shape each half into a 2 inch wide log. Transfer the logs to the cookie sheet. Bake until golden and firm to the touch, about 35 minutes or until a tester inserted in the center comes out clean. Cool the logs about 20 minutes on the cookie sheet. Reduce the oven temperature to 325°F.

Put the logs on a cutting board, discarding the wax paper. Cut each log diagonally into 1/2 inch slices. Arrange the slices flat side down on the cookie sheet. Bake at 325°F until crisp and golden, about 15 minutes. Transfer the biscotti to racks to cool completely.

Makes: Approximately 45

MANGO

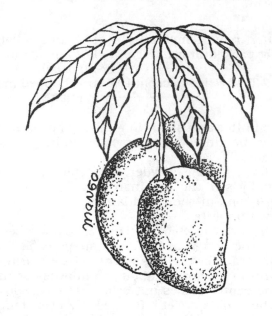

The mango, *mangifera indica*, is often called "the peach of the tropics". Interestingly, this savory exotic fruit belongs to a large group of trees and shrubs called *anacardiaceae*, which include the cashew nut tree, poison ivy, and poison sumac! That's why some people get "mango rash" if they eat raw mangos which are not properly peeled or washed.

Sometimes the mango has been described as a combination of a peach, pineapple, and apricot. Whatever you believe the taste to be, to eat a velvety and juicy fresh mango is an unforgettable experience.

A native of Southeast Asia, the mango has been cultivated and praised since ancient times. The Persians are said to have brought the fruit to East Africa in the 10th century. In the 16th century, the mango was introduced to Brazil and the West Indies...and as they say, the rest is history!

Mangos normally reach maturity 4-5 months after flowering. The yield varies with the age of the tree. At 10-20 years, a good crop may be 200 or more fruits per tree. Washing the fruit after harvest is not only essential to remove poisons, but it will prevent leaking sap from burning the skin and making black lesions which lead to rotting. To choose a good mango, make sure it has a floral scent. It should give slightly to the touch if it is ripe. You also need to make sure the fruit is not too soft and is not bruised.

It is often a struggle to remove the seed from the mango. The flesh does not leave the large central pit without a fight! The fruit should be cut in half with a knife as near to the large black pit as possible, then given a slight twist to free it.

For salads or desserts, the halves can be peeled and sliced. If you want to eat the mango raw, score each half into one inch divisions without cutting the skin. Then, turn each half inside out and you have a bunch of bite size pieces. Central Americans love to eat mangos this way, sprinkled with lime and salt.

Over 500 varieties of the mango have evolved. Mangos vary in size and shape, but usually resemble a large avocado. The skin can be green, yellow, orange, red, purple, or a combination thereof. The soft and juicy flesh is yellow, orange, or reddish in color. Mango pulp is slippery, sometimes fibrous. Big fleshy mangos called "*mangas*" can be found in Central America, but the smaller, thinner skinned varieties are the best purchases.

In addition to eating mangos raw, they may be preserved as jam, canned, made into syrup and nectar, utilizcd in sauces and chutney, and used to flavor ice cream.

ISLAND CHICKEN AND TROPICAL FRUIT SALAD
Ensalada de Las Islas Tropicales

1/2 cup dry white wine
1/2 tsp. salt
1 T. black peppercorns
1 lime
5 sprigs thyme
1 to 1 1/2 chicken breasts (about
   1 lb.) without bone and skin

1/2 ripe mango
1/2 ripe small papaya
1 bunch watercress, rinsed,
   large stems trimmed
2 slices lime
1/2cups Curry Mayonnaise*
(see recipe next page)

63

In a large saucepan combine the wine, salt, peppercorns, juice of half the lime, and thyme springs. Add the chicken breast and enough water to cover. Heat the liquid to a boil, and skim off any scum that forms. Reduce the heat, and simmer for 10 minutes. Remove the pan from the heat, and allow the chicken to cool in the liquid for 45 minutes.

Meanwhile, peel the papaya and mango, and rub them with the other lime half. Slice each into 1/2 inch wedges, and sprinkle with lime juice.

Cut the chicken breasts lengthwise into 6 slices.

Arrange the watercress on two individual serving plates. Alternate slices of mango, papaya, and chicken in a fan pattern on the watercress. Garnish with a slice of lime and dollops of the curry mayonnaise. This is a dazzling luncheon salad.

Serves: 2

*Curry Mayonnaise...a perfect dressing for chicken or seafood salads!

1 T. safflower oil	juice of 1 lime
1/2 onion, finely chopped	2 T. sour cream
2 T. curry powder	2 T. mango chutney
1 cup mayonnaise	

Heat the oil in a small skillet. Add the onion and saute over low heat until soft, 8 to 10 minutes. Add the curry powder and cook, stirring, 5 minutes. Set aside and allow to cool thoroughly.

When they are cool, combine the curried onions with the mayonnaise, lime juice, sour cream, and chutney. Stir well. Refrigerate until ready to serve.

Makes: 1 1/2 cups

MANGO, BLACK BEAN AND SHRIMP SALAD
Ensalada de Mango, Frijoles Negros, y Camarones

Shrimp and Marinade:

12 jumbo shrimp, peeled with tails intact and deveined	1 T. fresh lime juice
	1/2 tsp. ground coriander
1 T. extra-virgin olive oil	Salt and pepper to taste

Salad:

1 ripe mango	4 scallions, trimmed and minced
2 cups firm-cooked black beans (See instructions under "Beans")	2 T. fresh lime juice
4 T. finely chopped mint leaves or 1 T. dried mint	2 T. extra-virgin olive oil
	Salt and pepper to taste

Prepare the shrimp and marinade: Combine the shrimp, olive oil, lime juice, coriander, and salt and pepper in a shallow bowl and toss to mix. Cover and marinate in the refrigerator for 30 minutes.

If grilling, preheat the grill to very hot, or if broiling, preheat the broiler with the rack 3 inches from the heat. Grill or broil the shrimp until cooked, about 1 minute per side, basting with the marinade. Let the shrimp cool.

Meanwhile, prepare the salad: Peel and seed the mango. Cut it into 1/2 inch diced pieces. Cook the black beans as instructed on p. 141 (The recipe can be prepared ahead to this stage.)

Not more than 10 minutes before serving, combine the mango, black beans, 3 tablespoons of mint leaves, the scallions, olive oil, lime juice, salt and pepper in a mixing bowl and toss to mix. Correct the seasonings, adding salt or lime juice to taste. The salad should be highly seasoned.

Mound the black bean mixture on 4 plates. Arrange 3 shrimp on top of each, tails to the center, raised like a tripod. Sprinkle the shrimp with the remaining mint and serve at once as a light lunch salad or a first course.

Serves: 4

LIZETTE'S MANGO BREAD
Pan de Mango de Lizette

2 cups all purpose flour
2 tsp. baking soda
2 tsp. ground cinnamon
1/2 tsp. salt
1 cup vegetable oil
1 cup granulated or brown sugar

3 eggs, lightly beaten
1 tsp. vanilla
2 cups cubed ripe mangos
1/4 cup golden raisins
3 T. shredded coconut

Grease and flour a loaf pan. Sift together the flour, baking soda, cinnamon, and salt.

In a large mixing bowl beat together the vegetable oil and sugar, blending well. Gradually stir in the flour mixture, alternating with the eggs. Beat in the vanilla extract. Stir in the mango. Fold in the raisins and coconut.

Pour the batter into the loaf pan and set aside to rest for 20 minutes, or until the batter bubbles. In an oven preheated to 350°F, bake for 45 to 60 minutes. Remove the bread from the pan and cool on a rack.

Slice the bread and serve plain or topped with vanilla ice cream.

Makes: 1 loaf

TROPICAL CHICKEN
Pollo Tropical

1 chicken (3 1/2 to 4 lbs.), cut
   into 8 even-size pieces
Salt and black pepper to taste
1 T. vegetable oil
2 T. unsalted butter
1/4 cup finely chopped shallots
1 clove garlic, minced
1 T. finely chopped candied ginger
   or fresh ginger

2 cups coconut milk, fresh or
   unsweetened canned
1/4 cup orange marmalade,
   or to taste
1 cup diced fresh papaya
1 cup diced fresh mango
1 cup diced fresh pineapple
1/2 cup cashews, lightly
   toasted*
1/4 cup toasted coconut*

*To toast the cashews and the shredded coconut, spread them on baking sheets, place in a 350°F preheated oven, and brown, stirring frequently for about 5 to 8 minutes.

Wash the chicken and blot dry with paper towels. Season with salt and pepper. Heat the oil in a large saute pan. Brown the chicken on all sides, 3 to 4 minutes.

Melt the butter in the pan. Saute the shallots, garlic, and ginger until soft but not brown, about 2 minutes. Return the chicken to the pan and stir in the coconut milk, marmalade, and salt and pepper.

Simmer the chicken, uncovered, until almost cooked, 15 to 20 minutes. Stir in the fresh fruits and the cashews, and cook the chicken through, about 5 minutes more. Correct the seasonings, adding salt and pepper to taste. If the sauce needs sweetness, add a little more orange marmalade.

Transfer the chicken to a bowl or platter and spoon the sauce and fruit over it. Sprinkle the toasted coconut on top and serve at once.

Serves: 4

MANGO-BLACKBERRY PIE
Pie de Mango y Mora

Filling:
5 cups sliced ripe mangos
2 cups blackberries or raspberries,
   rinsed and drained
1/3 cup granulated sugar,
   firmly packed

1/3 cup brown
   sugar, firmly packed
5 T. all purpose flour
2 T. lime juice

Pastry Dough:
2 cups flour
3/4 tsp. salt

2/3 cup shortening
4 to 6 T. ice water

Pastry Dough:
2 cups flour   2/3 cup shortening
3/4 tsp. salt   4 to 6 T. ice water

In a mixing bowl, combine the mangos and the berries. Sprinkle with the granulated and brown sugar, flour, and lime juice. Gently mix to coat, and set aside.

To make the pastry dough, combine 2 cups flour with salt . Cut the shortening into small pea-sized pieces, then add it to the mixture. Drizzle in 4 to 6 tablespoons ice water, and mix with a fork to form a ball. Wrap the dough in plastic wrap and flatten it into a 6 inch disk. Chill for at least 20 minutes or until the next day.

With a rolling pin, flatten the chilled pastry dough into a 14 inch round. Place in a 9 inch pie pan, letting the pastry drape over the edge. Spoon the fruit mixture into the pastry shell. Fold the draped pastry over the center to cover the fruit. Pinch the pastry around the rim of the pie. Bake in a 350°F oven until the crust is golden, about 1 hour.

Serves: 8

MANGO UPSIDE DOWN CAKE
Queque Volteado de Mango

3 cups firm, ripe mango, cut   1 tsp. baking powder
   into slices   1 cup flour
1/2 stick of butter   1/4 tsp. salt
3/4 cup brown sugar   3 eggs
1/4 cup water   1 cup granulated sugar
1/4 cup milk

Melt the butter in a saucepan. Add the brown sugar and water. Cook, stirring constantly, for about 5 minutes. until bubbling. Add the mango slices and cook five more minutes. Pour into a round 9-inch cake pan and cool.

Combine the flour, salt, and baking powder. Put aside. In a separate bowl, beat the eggs with the sugar until light and fluffy. Fold the dry ingredients into the egg mixture, and add 1/4 cup of milk. Pour into the cake pan over the mango mixture. Bake for 35 minutes at 350° F.

Serves: 6 to 8

ORANGE/NARANJA

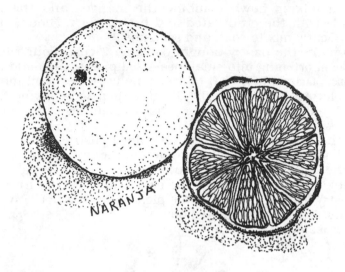

NARANJA

The orange, *citrus sinensis*, naranja in Spanish, needs no introduction. It's the world's most important citrus fruit, and there are many varieties. The origins of the orange are unknown. The assumption is the fruit originated in Asia and was carried to the Mediterranean area either by Italian traders or Portuguese navigators. The Spanish undoubtedly introduced the orange to this region.

Oranges grow on medium-size evergreen trees which may yield 100 fruits or more in a growing season. The fruits are borne from clusters of sweet, fragrant white flowers. After puncturing it, the thick leathery peel of the fruit is easily removed revealing wedge-shaped segments. Not only is the fruit utilized in cooking, but grated peel (zest) is used as a flavoring.

The orange is very durable and can be stored for a long time, however, it is subject to fungal diseases and mold. Newcomers to Costa Rica will find the peel of the fruit is usually not orange!! The peel can vary from green to yellow with brown blemishes which are not indicative of a bad orange. Local oranges seem to be better suited to the making of juice than to eating their granular sections raw. Cousins like the *tangerina* (tangerine) or *mandarina* (mandarin orange) are better selections for dishes calling for orange wedges.

Oranges are commonly peeled, segmented, and used in fruit cups, salads, gelatins, and desserts. They are also employed as garnishes and in the preparation of jams and jellies. Dried orange slices and orange peel can be candied as confections.

ORANGE SYRUP
Miel de Naranja

5 to 6 oranges, enough to make 2 cups of juice
Honey to taste

Squeeze the oranges to make 2 cups juice. Strain the juice into a nonreactive heavy saucepan. Briskly simmer the juice until thick and reduced to about 1/2 cup, 5 to 8 minutes. Add honey to taste. Cover and store the orange syrup in the refrigerator.

This syrup is similar to commercial concentrated orange juice, but without its bitterness. It will keep several weeks in the refrigerator or can be frozen. The syrup can be added to a variety of sauces, salad dressings, and desserts.

Makes: 1/2 cup

SHRIMP CEVICHE
Ceviche de Camarones

2 lbs. small to medium raw shrimp
Juice from 8 oranges (1 cup to
  1 1/2 cups)
Juice from 4 limes (1/2 cup)
3 medium onions, sliced and
  passed through hot water
1/2 cup chopped parsley

2 large tomatoes, seeded,
  and finely chopped
1 tsp. fresh chiles, chopped
  (use jalapeño or panama)
2 T. olive oil
2 T. catsup

Mix all the liquid ingredients. Remove the shells from the shrimp and parboil for about 3-4 minutes, until they turn slightly pink. Add the shrimp, onions, chilies, tomatoes, and parsley to the liquid ingredients. Refrigerate. This can be done up to 3 hours before serving.

Serves: 6 to 8

TRIPLE "O" SALAD
Ensaladaa de Tres "O"

3 large oranges
1 medium white or red onion
12 to 18 black olives, sliced
4 oz. any type blue-veined cheese
   (gorgonzola or blue cheese)
Salt and pepper to taste

3 T. red wine vinegar
12 butter lettuce leaves,
   washed and crisped
1 clove garlic, minced
6 T. olive oil

Peel the oranges, removing all white membrane. Cut crosswise into thin slices. In a large mixing bowl, combine the orange slices with the onions and olives.

In a small bowl, mash the cheese with a fork, mix in the garlic, and add the olive oil and vinegar. Pour this sauce over the orange mixture, and refrigerate.

Line six salad plates with the lettuce leaves, and spoon the salad atop the lettuce. Season with salt and pepper.

Serves: 6

CARROT AND ORANGE SOUP
Sopa de Zanahoria y Naranja

4 T. sweet butter
2 cups finely chopped onion
12 carrots (1 1/2 to 2 lbs.),
   peeled and chopped

4 cups chicken stock
1 cup fresh orange juice
salt and pepper to taste
grated fresh orange zest

Melt the butter in a pot. Add the onions, cover, and cook over low heat until tender and lightly colored, about 30 minutes. Add carrots and stock and bring to a boil. Reduce heat, cover, and simmer until carrots are very tender, about 25 minutes.

Pour the soup through a strainer and transfer the solids to the bowl of a food processor fitted with a steel blade, or use a food mill fitted with a medium disc. Add 1 cup of the cooking stock and process until smooth.

Return puree to the pot and add the orange juice and additional stock, 2 to 3 cups, until soup is of desired consistency. Season to taste with salt and pepper. Add orange zest to taste. Simmer until heated through and serve.

Serves: 4 to 6

ORANGE BRUNCH CAKE
Queque de Naranja para Brunch

8 T. (1 stick) sweet butter, softened
3/4 cup granulated sugar
2 eggs, separated
grated zest of 2 oranges
1 1/2 cups unbleached flour

1 1/2 tsp. baking powder
1/4 tsp. baking soda
1/4 tsp. salt
1/2 cup fresh orange juice
Orange Glaze

Orange Glaze:
1/4 cup fresh orange juice   1/4 cup granulated sugar

Combine orange juice and sugar in a small saucepan and simmer gently for 5 minutes, stirring occasionally, until a light syrup forms.

Preheat oven to 350°F. Grease a 10-inch bundt pan.

Cream the butter and gradually add the sugar, beating until light. Beat in egg yolks, one at a time, and the orange zest.

Sift the flour with baking powder, baking soda and salt. Add dry ingredients alternately with the orange juice to the batter. Beat the egg whites until stiff and fold them into the batter.

Pour batter into the prepared bundt pan. Bake for 30 to 35 minutes, or until sides of the cake shrink away from edges of pan and a cake tester, inserted in the center comes out clean.

Cool for 10 minutes in pan, unmold onto a rack, and drizzle with Orange Glaze while warm. Cool before serving.

Serves: 8 to 10

PAPAYA

The papaya, *carica papaya*, is native to Southern Mexico and Central America. Papaya "trees", which are really soft-wooded, palm-like plants, bear fruit the year around, thus papayas are always found in Central American markets. Most plants will ripen 2-4 fruits per week during the fruiting period.

The fruit is usual oval in shape and can weight from a few ounces to 20 pounds or more. The papaya is a melon-like fruit with a yellow to deep orange pulp and a cavity full of black seeds. If one chooses to utilize them,.the seeds are edible and make a dramatic garnish.

Two papaya varieties are common in Costa Rica. The *Amarilla* papaya with its yellow-orange skin is somewhat rounder than the more elongated red-orange *Cacho* papaya. People either love or dislike the papaya...some find it rather tasteless.

A ripe papaya will always be soft, but buyers should avoid too-soft papayas and fruits with musky odors. Usually vendors will cut the papaya open to show buyers the pulp color. Frequently, because of its size, the fruit is sold by the half. After scooping the seeds raw with a little lime juice. It can also be used in combination with other fruits in salads and to make *batidos*.

Because of its latex context, unripe green papaya cannot be eaten raw. It is boiled until tender, then served as a vegetable or mixed into a vegetable soup. The green fruit contains papain, a protein-digesting enzyme, which is used commercially as a meat tenderizer.

PAPAYA SEED DRESSING
Aderezo de Semillas de Papaya

1 heaping T. onion, finely chopped
1/4 tsp. ground black pepper
1/2 tsp. grated fresh ginger
1/2 tsp. salt
1 small clove garlic
1 tsp. fresh or dried tarragon
1/2 tsp dry mustard
2 T. papaya seeds
1 T. lime juice
1 cup salad oil

Put all ingredients in a blender and blend at high speed until smooth and the papaya seeds are the coarseness of black ground pepper.

Serve over avocado, papaya and hearts of palm on a bed of crisp lettuce leaves.

Makes: approxmately 1 1/4 cups

PAPAYA SALSA
Salsa de Papaya

2 ripe papayas (about 1 lb. each)
1 jalapeño or serrano pepper
1 large clove garlic, finely minced
1/2 cup freshly chopped red onion

1/4 cup coarsley chopped
  cilantro
Grated zest of 2 limes
1/2 cup lime juice

Peel the papayas, remove the seeds, and cut the pulp into 1/4 to 1/2 inch cubes. Place them in a medium-size bowl.

Carefully seed and finely chop the pepper. You should have about 1 tablespoon. Add it to the papaya, along with the remaining ingredients. Toss together gently. Serve this salsa within 4 to 5 hours for a really fresh taste.

The salsa adds a festive note to snapper or sea bass, grilled chicken or grilled shrimp.

Makes: 1 quart

PAPAYA AND AVOCADO COCKTAIL
Coctel de Papaya y Aguacate

1/2 cup unsweetened pineapple
  juice
1 tsp. chili powder
2 T. salad oil
1 1/2 T. lime juice

1/8 tsp. ground nutmeg
1 each, papaya and avocado
  (enough to make 4 cups)
4 strips of bacon, cooked,
  drained and crumbled

Combine the pineapple juice, chili powder, oil, lime juice, and nutmeg. Set aside. Cut the papaya into chunks. Cut the avocado in half, cross-wise, pit and peel, and slice. Combine it with the papaya in a medium size bowl. Pour the dressing over it, and chill the mixture for at least 1 hour. To serve, arrange in cups or on plates and sprinkle with the crumbled bacon.

Serves: 4 to 6

PAPAYA AND BLACK BEAN SALSA
Salsa de Papaya y Frijoles Negros

8 oz. ripe papaya, peeled, seeded,
1 cup Firm Cooked Black Beans
1/2 cup finely chopped red onion
2 T. minced fresh ginger
1/2 scotch bonnet chili, or to taste
   or 2 jalapeño chiles, seeded
   & minced

2 tsp. minced fresh ginger
1/4 cup chopped cilantro
3 T. lime juice, or to taste
1 T. extra-virgin olive oil
1 T. (packed) light brown
   sugar (optional)
Salt and pepper to taste

Combine all of the ingredients in a mixing bowl, and gently toss to mix. Correct the seasonings, adding salt, lime juice, or brown sugar to taste. The salsa should be a little sweet and a little sour.

The salsa makes a good accompaniment to roasted chicken or grilled fish, and is best served within a couple of hours of making. Refrigerate, covered, until serving time.

Serves: 4

AVOCADO, PAPAYA, CHICKEN SALAD
Ensalada de Aguacate, Papaya, y Pollo

1 cup plain yogurt
1/4 cup mango chutney,
   finely chopped
1 T. lime juice
3 cups shredded cooked chicken
8 butter lettuce leaves, washed
   and crisped

1 medium papaya (1 lb.),
   peeled, seeded, and sliced
2 firm medium avocados,
   peeled, pitted, and sliced
1/2 cup macadamias,
   chopped and toasted

Combine the yogurt, chutney, and lemon juice to make a dressing. Mix 3/4 of the dressing with the chicken.

Line four salad plates with the lettuce and mound 1/4 of the chicken mixture on each plate. Arrange the papaya and avocado slices over the chicken salad. Spoon the remaining dressing on top and garnish with the macadamias.

Serves: 4

SEA BASS WITH PAPAYA
Corvina con Papaya

1 lb. ripe papaya
1 lb. sea bass fillets
1/4 cup fresh lime juice and
　　white wine (half & half)
1/4 tsp. salt

1/3 cup flour
1/4 cup margarine
1 T. vegetable oil
Pinch of cinnamon
1 T. brown sugar

Cut the papaya length-wise, scoop out the seeds, pare, and cut into 1/2 inch slices. Sprinkle the sea bass with 1 tablespoon lime juice and let stand for 5 minutes. Then sprinkle the fish with salt and dip it in flour, shaking off the excess. Heat the oil and butter in a 12 inch frying pan, and fry the fish for 2 minutes on each side. Remove the fish from the pan and keep it warm.

Add two tablespoons of butter to the skillet, then the papaya. Sprinkle the papaya with cinnamon and cook it for about 1 minute. Arrange the papaya over the fish. Sprinkle the brown sugar into the skillet drippings and stir in the wine/lime mixture. Heat to a boil for about 2 minutes and spoon the sauce over the sea bass. Serve immediately.

Serves: 4

GREEN PAPAYA HASH
Picadillo de Papaya Verde

1 medium green papaya
1/2 lb. pork shoulder (posta),
　　cubed
2 tsp. dry mustard
1/2 lb. pork sausage (chorizo)
1/2 stick margarine
2 green peppers, minced
Salt and pepper to taste

1 bunch cilantro, chopped
1 medium onion, chopped
2 cloves of garlic, minced
1 celery rib, chopped
3 oregano leaves
2 T. powdered chicken broth
1 cup beef broth

Peel the papaya, and boil it until tender, but not overdone. Drain the papaya in a colander, then finely chop it. Add the meat, onion, and garlic to 2 cups of water with 2 tablespoons of powdered chicken broth. Cover and simmer until the meats are tender. Saute the onion, celery, garlic, and green pepper. Add the cubed meats and chopped papaya to 1 cup of beef broth. Serve with fresh tortillas.

Serves: 4

PASSION FRUIT/GRANADILLA & MARACUYA

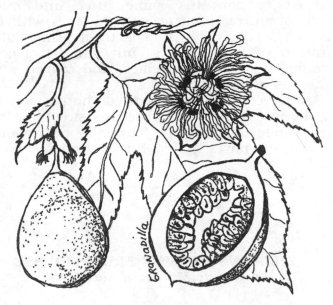

Granadilla is the Spanish name for passion fruit, *passiflora edulis*. There are over 500 species of passion fruit...and they widely differ in color and other characteristics. Granadillas range in color from purple to yellow and from the size of a lemon to that of a small melon. Included in the group is the giant granadilla, the sweet granadilla, the water lemon, the banana passion fruit, the sweet calabash, and the maracuyá.

The exact origin of the fruit is not known, but many species are thought to be native to tropical America. There are several stories about the origin of the English name. Since the flower has a multitude of ray-like filaments resembling Christ's crown, the name is said to be symbolic of Christ's passion. Others credit the name to the proported aphrodisiac properties of the fruit's flowers.

The granadillas found in local markets usually are lemon-sized with a smooth, brittle rind. The green rind lightens in color to yellow and takes on a purple blush as the fruit ripens. When the rind is cracked open, an orange, mucilaginous pulp with black crisp edible seeds is revealed. The flesh looks similar to that of a pomegranate. The pulp and seeds can be eaten out of hand or ground up and strained to make juice.

The maracuyá is a larger more oblong fruit. Its central cavity contains some juice and masses of yellowish or purple-pink sweet-acid pulp with flattened oval brown seeds. The pulp is used principally in the preparation of fruit drinks, but can be used in the preparation of sauces and jellies, and cooked with sugar and eaten as a dessert.

An aficionado has described the passion fruits as having the tartness of lime juice, the sweetness of honey, the fragrance of jasmine, and a perfumed flavor reminiscent of guava, lychee, and pineapple! Wow!

LILIANA'S PASSION FRUIT MOUSSE
Mousse de Maracuyá de Liliana

1 lb. maracuyá
1 cup plus 3 T. water
1/4 cup water
2 envelopes unflavored gelatin

1/2 cup sugar
1/2 cup evaporated milk
1(14 oz.) can condensed milk
4 egg whites

Sauce:
2 1/2 cups milk
1 T. cornstarch, dissolved in a
 little milk

1/2 cup sugar
4 egg yolks
1 tsp. vanilla

Cut the maracuyá in half and remove the seeds and rind. In a blender, blend the pulp with a small amount of water. Remove the liquid and strain it, making 2 cups strained juice. Add a little more water if less than 2 cups.

Dissolve the gelatin in 1/4 cup water in the microwave for 30 seconds. Cool. Blend the 2 cups of juice with 1/2 cup sugar and the milks. Add the gelatin and stir well for about 10 seconds.

In the blender, beat the egg whites until stiff, but not dry and very gently fold into the maracuyá mixture. Smear a chimney mold with a little egg white, add the mixture, and refrigerate for 6 hours or overnight.

To make the sauce: Mix all ingredients except the vanilla in a blender. Cook in a sauce pan over a medium heat, stirring constantly with a wooden spoon, until the mixture boils and thickens. Remove from the heat and add the vanilla. Cool, and refrigerate.

To serve, remove the mousse from the mold and place on a bed of lettuce. Pour the sauce over the mousse.
Serves: 6 to 8

ROBIN'S PASSION FRUIT PIE
Pie de Maracuyá de Robin

1 9-inch baked pie shell
1 cup sugar
1/3 cup cornstarch
1 1/4 cups water
3 egg yolks, beaten
3 T. margarine or butter

3/4 cup pure maracuyá juice
3 egg whites
1/2 tsp. vanilla
1/4 tsp. cream of tartar
6 T. sugar

Heat oven to 400°F. Mix sugar and cornstarch in a small saucepan. Stir in water gradually. Cook over medium heat, stirring constantly, until mixture thickens and boils. Boil and stir 1 minute. Stir at least half of the hot mixture gradually into the beaten egg yolks. Blend into the hot mixture in the saucepan. Boil and stir 1 minute. Remove from heat. Stir in margarine and maracuyá juice. Pour into pie shell.

Make meringue by beating egg whites and cream of tartar until foamy. Beat in sugar, 1 tablespoon at a time, continue beating until stiff and glossy. Do not underbeat. Beat in the vanilla.

Spoon meringue onto hot pie filling; spread over filling, carefully sealing meringue to edge of crust to prevent shrinking or weeping. Bake until delicate brown, about 10 minutes. Cool away from draft.
Serves: 8 to 10

PEACH PALM/PEJIBAYE

Like the coconut, the pejibaye, *bacstris gasipaes*, grows in clusters on a palm tree. Most English speaking people have never seen or heard of this fruit before coming to Costa Rica, however, it is native to Latin America and Costa Rica is the world's largest producer! The pejibaye provided the regions' indigenous peoples with food, drink, and shelter. They learned how to preserve it, make liquor from it, and use the stems for building materials.

Pejibayes hang in clusters of 50 to 100 or more fruits. A palm with 4 or 5 stems may produce up to 150 pounds of fruit in a single season. The pejibaye is a nut-like fruit, ovoid in shape, about the size of an egg. Its thin skin is yellow to orange, darkening in color as it ripens. Light orange flesh surrounds the large black pejibaye seed. The fruit is caustic in its natural state, so it is boiled, like a potato, before being eaten. After the fruit is cooled and the skin and seed removed, the pejibaye can be eaten out of hand. The fruit can be dry and somewhat fibrous, thus the practice of adding mayonnaise to the seed cavity before eating the pejibaye has evolved.

The flavor of the pejibaye is difficult to describe. Some say the flavor is a combination of a chestnut and a pumpkin while others feel the fruit has little flavor.

Pejibayes can be utilized a number of ways. They can be added to salads and casseroles. They can be ground and used in a powdery state to make dips and to add to various dishes. The fruit can be mixed with cornmeal, eggs, and milk and fried. Peeled, seeded, halved fruits are sometimes canned in brine and exported.

Pejibayes are very hearty. They can be kept in a dry location for a long, long time and when refrigerated can be kept uncooked for as long as 6 weeks before beginning to spoil. The pejibaye is an excellent source of vitamins, but beware, the average fruit contains 1000 or more calories!

HOT TIPS!

- For a snack, cut in half and put mayonnaise in the pit cavity.
- Marinate cooked pieces in a vinaigrette and serve cold.
- Mix in a blender equal amounts of cream cheese, mayonaise, and pejibaye. Season with salt and pepper to taste. Serve on crackers or dark bread.

PEJIBAYE CREAM SOUP
Crema de Pejibaye

20 cooked pejibayes	1 onion, minced
6 cups of chicken broth	4 T. flour
1 cup milk	3 bay leaves
1 cup cream	1/2 cup white wine
1/2 stick butter or margarine	Salt and pepper to taste

In a sauce pan saute the onion in butter until it crystallizes. Add the flour, then the chicken broth, stirring constantly until the mixture thickens. Cook the pejibayes and puree them in a blender. Add the pejibaye puree and the bay leaves to the mixture. Cover and simmer for 30 minutes.

When ready to serve, remove the bay leaves, put the mixture, little by little, into a blender, adding the wine and cream. Return the soup to a sauce pan and reheat before serving.

Serves: 6 to 8

PEJIBAYE MOUSSE
Mousse de Pejibaye

1 pkg. of cream cheese (115 gm.)
1/4 cup mayonnaise
3 envelopes gelatin, dissolved in
    2 cups hot chicken broth
15 pejibayes, cooked and peeled

2 T. finely chopped onions
1/2 cup chopped celery
1/2 cup whipping cream
1/2 cup pimentos, chopped

Buy 2 jars of cooked pejibayes, or if cooking fresh pejibayes, put them in a pot with enough water to cover, and add 3 tablespoons shortening, 1 tablespoon salt, and 3 tablespoons of brown sugar. Cover and cook until soft, about 45 minutes to an hour.

Puree the pejibayes in a blender. In a mixing bowl, mix the cream cheese and the mayonnaise, then add the pejibaye puree, the gelatin broth, and the other ingredients. Do not over mix. Put the mixture into a jello mold or a loaf pan and chill for four hours or overnight.

Serve the mousse on crackers or on lettuce as a first course.

Serves: 4 to 6 as a first course

GLAZED PEJIBAYES
Pejibayes Glaseados

2 lbs. pejibayes, cooked
    and peeled
6 T. butter

3/4 cup brown sugar
1 tsp. grated lime peel
1/2 tsp. ground ginger

Slice the pejibayes. Lightly saute in hot butter at medium heat. Sprinkle the brown sugar over the pejibaye slices. Add lime peel and ginger. Stir with a wooden spoon until the pejibayes are glazed.

Make the dish just before serving so the pejibayes retain their luster. Serve as a side dish with meat, poultry, or fish.

Serves: 6

PINEAPPLE/PINA

Piña

The pineapple, *ananas comosus*, of the *Bromeliaceae* family, is an important tropical fruit, well-known to both North Americans and Europeans. It's native to Southern Brazil and Paraguay. After the Amerindians domesticated the plant, the Spanish and Portuguese carried the pineapple up through South and Central America. Pineapples and their crowns became symbols of friendship and hospitality for the indigenous peoples. Europeans adopted the pineapple motif which was represented in doorway carvings in Spain, England, and later in Colonial New England.

This fruit grows on a central stalk, jutting out from a cactus-like plant. The oval shaped fruit has a spiny skin, the color of which can range from green to yellowish-orange, and is topped with a prickly short tuft. Upon maturation the fruit is cut from its stalk with a machete.

A small compact crown usually indicates a good quality pineapple; however, neither the skin or fruit color indicates ripeness. To test for ripeness, snap a finger against the side. A dull thud along with protruding scales and a sweet aroma indicate you have a good fruit. Unlike other fruits, the pineapple will not ripen further after harvesting. However, if kept too long, it will become soft and mushy.

The pineapple can be cut into rings, chunks or long wedges. When fresh, it is best eaten raw. Not only can it be eaten out of hand, it can be used in salads, compotes, and desserts. The pineapple is also used as a garnish on ham or can be prepared for sauces and preserves. In some regions, principally Southeast Asia, the pineapple is utilized in the preparation of curries and a number of meat dishes. Pineapple does not lend itself well to freezing. If it is not eaten fresh, it is usually canned or used to make beverages. Cut pineapple can be refrigerated up to one week.

To prepare the pineapple, grab the tuft at the top, and with a paring knife remove the skin by cutting diagonally from the top. The fruit can then be cut crosswise or into wedges. Or the pineapple may be prepared as a boat, leaving the outer skin, cutting it lengthwise, and removing the pulp.

TRY THESE!

- Melt a sharp cheese on thin pineapple slices and ham slices atop corn bread.
- Serve thinly sliced fresh pineapple on raisin bread or pumpernickel spread with cream cheese.
- Use our pineapple salsa with burritos!
- Cut the pineapple, with the skin attached, into fourths. Cut the fruit into pie-shaped wedges and re-insert into the boat. Let guests remove the wedges with toothpicks or small forks.
- Wrap pineapple spears with bacon and broil under a moderate heat.

PINEAPPLE SALSA
Salsa de Piña

1 1/2 cups pineapple, chopped
1 T. chopped cilantro
1 T. fresh lime juice

1 T. sugar
1 tsp. minced fresh ginger
Fresh black pepper, to taste

Stir all the ingredients together, cover, and chill until ready to serve. Will keep in the refrigerator for up to 2 days.

This salsa is a great topping for simply prepared fish, fish cakes, grilled poultry...and even roasted duck!

Makes: 1 1/2 cups

PINEAPPLE--PAPAYA CHUTNEY
Chutney de Piña y Papaya

3 cups pineapple chunks,
  1/2 inch in size
1/2 fresh lime--peeled, seeded
  and chopped
1 1/4 cups white vinegar
1 medium onion, finely chopped
2 garlic cloves, minced
2 hot green peppers, finely minced
1/4 cup slivered ginger
1/2 cup seedless raisins

1/2 papaya--cut in 1/2"
  pieces
1 cup brown sugar, firmly
  packed
1 tsp. cinnamon
1/2 tsp. salt
1/4 tsp. ground cloves
1/4 tsp. ground allspice
1/4 tsp. ground red pepper
1/4 cup fresh lemon juice

Combine all the ingredients, except the fresh lime juice, in a large heavy sauce pan. Bring to a boil. Reduce the heat and simmer for an hour, stirring frequently.   Stir in the lime juice and simmer an additional 5 minutes. Cool before serving.

Makes: 4 cups

PINEAPPLE CABBAGE SLAW
Ensalada de Piña y Repollo

l cup chopped fresh pineapple
2 cups shredded cabbage
1/2 cup shredded onion

l cup vinegar
1/2 cup olive oil
Pinch of oregano, salt,
  pepper, and sugar

Shred the cabbage and pour 4 cups of boiling water over it. Let it soak for five minutes. Drain it well, then mix in the other ingredients. Chill the slaw for at least 2 hours or overnight before serving.

Serves: 6

SILVER PALATE CARROT CAKE
Gueque de Zanahorias

2 cups unbleached all-purpose flour
2 cups granulated sugar
2 tsp. baking soda
2 tsp. ground cinnamon
1 cup corn oil
3 eggs, lightly beaten
Confectioner's sugar, for dusting
*Cream Cheese Frosting (See the following recipe)

2 T. vanilla extract
1 1/3 cups pureed cooked
   carrots
1 cup chopped walnuts
1 cup shredded coconut
2/4 cup canned crushed
   pineapple, drained

Believe it or not, Central Americans love carrot cake! We have taken this one from the *Silver Palate Cookbook*. Serve it without the frosting for breakfast.

Preheat the oven to 350°F. Line a 13 x 9 inch layer cake pan with waxed paper, and grease the paper.

Sift the flour, sugar, baking soda, and cinnamon together in a large bowl. Add the oil, eggs, and vanilla, and beat well. Then fold in the carrots, walnuts, coconut, and pineapple.

Pour the batter into the prepared pan. Place it on the middle rack of the oven and bake until the edges have pulled away from the sides of the pan and a toothpick inserted in the center comes out clean, 1 hour.

Cool the cake in the pan for 10 minutes. Then invert it over a cake rack and unmold, remove the waxed paper, and continue to cool for 1 hour.

Frost the top and sides of the cooled cake with the cream cheese frosting, and then dust the top with confectioners' sugar.

Serves: 12

Cream Cheese Frosting

4 oz. cream cheese
1 1/2 cups confectioners' sugar
Juice of 1/4 lime

3 T. unsalted butter
1/2 tsp. vanilla extract

At room temperature, cream the cream cheese and butter together in a mixing bowl. Slowly sift in the confectioners' sugar, and continue beating until full incorporated. There should be no lumps. Stir in the vanilla and lemon juice.

PLANTAIN/PLATANO

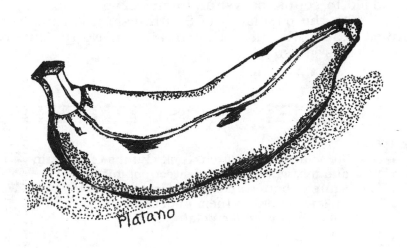

Platano

    The plantain, *platano* in Spanish, is a jumbo cousin of the banana. It is from the same family; it looks like a banana and smells like a banana, but don't treat the plantain like a banana...or you'll be in trouble! The plantain is a vegetable-like fruit. It can be eaten ripe or unripe, but it cannot be eaten raw. It must be fried, boiled, or baked.

    When green, the plantain is bland and starchy, like a yuca or a potato. As it ripens the plantain becomes sweeter. Green plantains will have a green peel, but real ripe ones will be almost totally black, yet the fruit remains firm. They're best when they look like you would want to throw them out! It will take 6-8 days for green plantains to fully ripen.

    Plantains are much more difficult than bananas to peel. With a paring knife, you should cut off the ends and cut the fruit into sections, the length you desire. Then make a lengthwise slit in the skin of each section. Slide your thumbnails under the slit to pry off the skin. Should this be difficult, soak the section in a bowl of ice water before skinning.

Plantains are an important starchy food in the Central American diet. *Tostones*, *maduros*, and other plantain preparations are as popular as french fries in the States, and they accompany many dishes. Plantains are an ingredient in many tasty Latin dishes. They can be added to soups, stews, and omelets.

With the popularity of Southwestern cuisine in the United States, the use of plantains in North American cooking has grown.

HOT TIPS!

- For your meal's starch, cook chunks of plantain and mix with apple and sweet potatoes.
- Saute in butter, then sprinkle with brown sugar and brown them under the broiler.
- Bake and mash like potatoes.

GREEN PLANTAIN CEVICHE
Ceviche de Platano Verde

4 green plantains   1/2 cup vinegar
2 bell peppers, chopped   1/8 cup lime juice
2 medium onions, minced   3/4 cup olive oil
1 bunch cilantro, chopped   salt and pepper

Peel the plantains and cook in salted water. Drain and finely mince. Mix with the cilantro, onions, and bell pepper.

Whisk together the olive oil, lemon juice, vinegar, salt and pepper. Pour into the plantain mixture and mix well. Marinate at least one day before serving. Can be kept in the refrigerator for 3 or 4 days.

This ceviche can be served with hot, soft tortillas or tortilla chips as an appetizer. To serve as a first course, line salad plates with lettuce and top with the ceviche.

Serves: 8

FRIED PLANTAINS
Maduros

2 very ripe plantains   (about 1 pound total)
About one cup canola oil or other vegetable oil

Cut the plantains crosswise into 2 1/2 inch pieces. Make a lengthwise cut in each and peel off the skin as directed above. Cut each piece diagonally into 1/2 slices. Pour the oil to a depth of 1/2 inch in a heavy frying pan and heat to 350°f. Add the plantain slices and fry until crusty and golden brown, about one minute per side. Transfer the plantains to paper towels to drain. Serve at once.

Serves: 4

PLANTAIN CHIPS
Tostones

2 green plantains (1 lb.)

Herbed Salt:
1/2 tsp. dried oregano
1/2 tsp. garlic powder

2 cups olive oil (approx.)
or other cooking oil

1/2 tsp. dried thyme
1/2 tsp. salt

Cut the plantains crosswise into 2 1/2 inch pieces. Peel as described above, then cut diagonally into 1/2 inch slices. Pour the oil to a depth of 1/2 inch in a heavy frying pan and heat to 325°F. Add the plantain slices and fry until soft, about 2 minutes on each side. Transfer with a slotted spoon to paper towels to drain.

Mix the ingredients for the herb salt in a small mixing bowl. Just before serving, reheat the oil to 375°F. Using a tostone maker, tortilla press , or a meat pounder, flatten each plantain slice until 1/8 to 1/4 thick. (The thinner the tostone, the crisper it will be!)

Fry the tostones until crisp and golden brown, about a minute per side. Drain on paper towels, sprinkle with the herbed salt, and serve at once.

Serves: 4

GREEN PLANTAIN DUMPLING SOUP
Sopa de Albondigas de Platano Verde

6 green plantains
1/4 stick of margarine
1 whole egg
1/2 lb. cheese, grated
   (Turrialba or Monterey Jack)
8 cups chicken broth
2 medium potatoes, cubed
1/4 cup of cooking oil

3 medium carrots, cubed
3 medium chayotes, peeled
   and chopped
1 celery rib, finely chopped
1 bell pepper, finely chopped
1 medium onion, chopped
1/2 cup chopped cilantro
   Salt to taste

Peel the plantains and boil in water until soft. Remove from the water and mash by hand. Add the margarine, egg yolk, salt, and grated cheese. Mix well and form small 1" balls. Heat 1/4 cup oil in frying pan. Add the plantain balls, cooking until golden. Put on paper towels to remove the grease. In a stock pot, fry the onions, celery, bell pepper, and cilantro. Add the cubed vegetables and boil in the chicken broth until fork tender. Add the plantain balls when ready to serve.

Serves: 10

HEAVENLY PLANTAINS
Plantanos en Gloria

3 large ripe plantains
1 cup ground beef
1 clove garlic, finely minced
1 small onion, finely chopped
1 tomato chopped
6 capers, minced

1 T. minced parsley
1/2 cup red wine
1/2 cup water
1/4 cup tomato sauce
1 1/2 cups grated Mozzarella
Salt and Pepper

Peel the plantains and cut in half lengthwise. Fry until golden and remove from the heat. Saute the meat with the other ingredients, then add the wine and other liquids. With the fried plantains, make a layer in a pyrex dish. Pour the meat mixture on top. Sprinkle the grated cheese. Bake in a 350°F oven for 20 minutes. Serve with rice and fresh cream.

Serves: 6

STARFRUIT/CARAMBOLA

Carambola

The carambola, *averrhoa carambola*, is the ultimate aesthetic fruit! It's known in English as the Starfruit because when sliced crosswise, the fruit produces perfect 5 point stars!

The fruit is of Indochinese origin, most probably Malaysia--*carambola* is the Hindu word for fruit. The carambola tree grows in the hotter coastal regions of Central America where fruit production is often so prolific that tree limbs need support.

Both the skin and the flesh of this waxy surfaced fruit are golden yellow when ripe. Carambolas range from 3 to 5 inches long and are easy to identify by the five definitive ribs that traverse their length. The pulp is crisp and has a grape-like succulence, while the core is occasionally dotted with dark seeds. Cambolas do not require peeling...just wash and slice them!

The flavor, depending on the variety, can be exotically sweet to refreshingly tart. Generally, the broader set the ribs, the sweeter the fruit. It's best to look for the larger so-called "sweet" carambolas which are much less acidic than the smaller fruits.

Costa Ricans utilize the carambola primarily in delicious fruit drinks and in the preparations of jams and relishes. However, the carambola became a culinary superstar in the United States during the 1980's. Pioneers of nouvelle cuisine discovered its attractiveness as a garnish for salads, fish, desserts, and a host of other items. You can use this fruit as you would a lemon!

When purchasing carambolas, look for crisp, heavy fruits with firm, fat ribs and a bright even color. Avoid those which are browned, limp, soft or oozing. When ripe, the fruit will be juicy and smell perfumy and fragrant. Green fruits can be ripened at room temperature. Ripe fruits will keep for up to two weeks under refrigeration.

COLESLAW WITH STARFRUIT
Ensalada de Repollo con Carambola

Dressing:

1/3 cup mayonnaise
3 T. sour cream
Salt and pepper to taste
1/4 cup Orange Syrup
 (See our recipe or use concentrated orange juice.)

2 T. fresh lime juice
2 T. black sesame seeds
 (Regular can be subsituted)

Salad:

1/2 green cabbage, cored and thinly shredded (5 to 6 cups)
1/2 red bell pepper, cored, seeded, and thinly sliced
1/2 yellow bell pepper, cored, seeded, and thinly sliced
1 poblano chili or 1/2 green bell pepper, cored, seeded, and sliced
1 jalapeño chili, seeded and minced
1 ripe mango, diced
2 carambolas , thinly sliced
2 carrots
1 bunch of scallions, trimmed and finely chopped
1/4 cup chopped cilantro leaves

Prepare the dressing: Whisk the mayonnaise and sour cream in a large mixing bowl until smooth. Whisk in the orange syrup, vinegar, lime juice, sesame seeds, and salt and pepper. Correct the seasonings, adding lime juice and salt to taste.

Stir in all of the remaining ingredients, reserving one of the sliced carambolas for garnish. Correct the seasonings, adding salt, pepper, or vinegar to taste. Decorate the salad with the reserved star fruit slices and serve at once.

Serves: 8

CHOCOLATE-ORANGE FONDUE WITH TROPICAL FRUITS
Fondue de Chocolate y Naranja con Frutas Tropicales

1/3 cup whipping cream
8 oz. bittersweet or semisweet
   chocolate, finely chopped

1 1/2 tsp. grated orange peel,
  (packed)
3 T. Grand Marnier or Salicsa
  Orange Liqueur

Accompaniments: carambolas, strawberries, mango chunks, banana slices, or other tropical fruits of your choice. Dried fruits like apricots, pineapple, and mixed fruit packages found in the supermarket can also be used as well as chunks of pound cake or angel food cake.

Bring the whipping and grated orange peel to a simmer in a heavy medium-size saucepan. Reduce the heat to low. Add the chopped chocolate and 1 tablespoon Grand Marnier. Whisk until the mixture is smooth. Remove the fondue from the heat and blend in the remaining 2 tablespoons Grand Marnier.

Transfer the fondue to a fondue pot, or place the pan of fondue on an electric hot plate. Either way, be sure the heat is low as too much heat will cause the chocolate to burn.

Serves: 4

FRIED CUSTARD SQUARES WITH STAR FRUIT
Leche frita con Carambola

Custard squares:
2 1/2 cups milk
cinnamon stick
1/2 cup carambola
5 large eggs
6 T. cornstarch

2/3 cup plus 1/4 cup sugar
1/2 tsp. salt
1 cup fine dry bread crumbs
1 1/2 tsp. ground cinnamon
1 cup all-purpose flour

Sauce:
1 1/2 cups water
1 cup firmly packed brown sugar
fresh lime juice to taste

1/2 cut plus 1 T. dark rum
1/4 cup carambola

vegetable oil for deep frying
2 carambolas sliced thin for a garnish

To make the custard squares:

Butter an 8-inch square baking pan.

In a heavy saucepan bring milk just to a boil with cinnamon stick and carambola and keep at a bare simmer 15 minutes. Pour hot milk through a sieve into a large glass measuring cup or heat proof pitcher.

In a bowl with an electric mixer beat together 3 eggs, cornstarch, 2/3 cup sugar, and salt and add hot milk in a stream, beating until smooth. Return custard to saucepan and bring to a boil, whisking constantly. (Custard may look curdled as it begins to thicken but will become smooth as it is boiled and whisked.) Boil the custard, whisking vigorously, 1 minute and remove the saucepan from the heat. Custard will be very thick and smooth.

Immediately pour custard into prepared baking pan, smoothing the top, and chill, surface covered with plastic wrap, until firm, about 1 1/2 hours. Cut custard into 2-inch squares.

In a small bowl whisk together bread crumbs, remaining 1/4 cup sugar, and ground cinnamon. In another small bowl lightly whisk remaining 2 eggs.

Have ready flour in a bowl and a tray lined with wax paper. Working with 1 custard square at a time, coat square with flour, shaking off excess, and then with egg, letting excess drip off. Coat square with bread crumb mixture, transferring as coated to tray. Chill squares, uncovered, 30 minutes.

To make sauce:

In a saucepan combine water, sugar, 1/2 cup rum, and carambola and simmer, uncovered, 15 minutes. Stir in remaining tablespoon rum and lime juice and pour mixture through a sieve into a glass measuring cup or heat proof pitcher.

Preheat oven to 325°F. and set on a rack in a shallow baking pan. In a heavy 12- to 14-inch skillet heat 1 1/2 inches oil over moderately high heat until it registers 375°F. on a deep-fat thermometer and fry squares in 3 batches until golden, about 15 seconds on each side. Carefully transfer squares as fried with a slotted spatula to rack to drain and keep warm in oven.

Onto each of 8 dessert plates pour 2 tablespoons sauce. Halve 12 custard squares diagonally and arrange 3 triangles on each plate. Garnish desserts with carambola.

Serves: 8

TAMARIND/TAMARINDO

Tamarindo

    The tamarind, *Tamarindus indica*, is the fruit of a massive tree native to tropical Africa, but introduced to India where it took its name "tamar hindi", the Indian word for date. Thus, the fruit is sometimes known as Indian date. The tamarind tree is now established in all tropical countries, and is subject to numerous myths and superstitions. Some African tribes venerate the tree as sacred. It is thought harmful to sleep or tie a horse under the tamarind, most likely because of the corrosive effect of fallen damp leaves.

    Tamarind fruits are encased in crescent-shaped, fuzzy brown seed pods. The fruit is sticky and fibrous in its natural state. After peeling the pod from the pulp, the fruit is usually sold in plastic wrapped packages. To utilize the tamarind in food preparation, the flesh must be turned into "water".

    The sweet-acid flavor of the tamarind has been described as a cross between lime juice and prunes. The tamarind is said to contain more acid and more sugar per volume than any other fruit. Here in Central America, the tamarind is much used in the preparation of natural fruit drinks.

The pulp can be made into jelly and jam and be used to flavor sherbet and ice cream. It is also used to make chutney, syrups and sauces and as a seasoning for rice, fish, and meat dishes. Interestingly, this fruit flavors some brands of Worcestershire and barbecue sauces.

Tamarind Pulp...

In a small saucepan, cover about 2 1/2 cups shelled tamarind pods (about 14 oz.) with water and bring to a boil. Cover, reduce heat, and simmer the tamarind gently, stirring frequently, until the pulp loosens and falls off the seeds, about 30 minutes. If the mixture becomes too thick, add more water to keep the tamarind pods barely covered.

Strain the mixture through a medium sieve into a bowl, pushing hard with the back of a spoon to extract as much pulp as possible. If the pulp does not measure about 1 1/2 cups, return the solids to the pan with water to barely cover and bring to a boil. Strain the tamarind again in the same manner to extract more pulp.

Tamarind pulp may be made 1 week ahead and refrigerated covered.

Makes: about 1 1/2 cups

TAMARIND MARINADE
Recaudo de Tamarindo

6 dried chipotle chiles (or similar fiery chiles), stemmed, seeded,
   and deveined (Use rubber gloves)

1 cup boiling water	2 T. corn oil
1 medium onion, sliced in	4 plum tomatoes
1/2 inch slices	10 garlic cloves
1 1/2 cups fresh tamarind pulp	1 T. coarse salt, or to taste

In a small skillet heat the oil over a moderately high heat until hot, but not smoking and using tongs, fry the chiles, 1 or 2 at a time, turning them, until puffed and just beginning to brown, about 10 seconds. (Do not let the chiles burn or the recaudo will be bitter.) Transfer the chiles as fried to a small bowl, letting the excess oil drip off. Add boiling water and soak the chiles, tossing occasionally, until soft, about 20 minutes.

Heat a flat iron griddle over a moderately low heat and pan-roast the onion, garlic, and tomatoes, turning them occasionally to ensure even roasting, until browned and soft throughout, 25 to 30 minutes. Discard the garlic skins and the tomato stems.

In a blender or food processor blend the chiles, 1/2 cup of the soaking water, onion, garlic, tomatoes, and tamarind pulp. Salt to taste.

This smoky, earthy marinade with a sweet-and sour tang can be used to flavor pork, beef, venison, or jumbo shrimp prior to grilling. It can be made up to 5 days ahead and refrigerated.

Makes: about 3 1/4 cups

PORK IN TAMARIND SAUCE
Cerdo en Salsa de Tamarindo

2 1/2 lbs. lean boneless pork,	1/4 cup vegetable oil
cut into 1 1/2 inch cubes	2 cups chicken broth
4 T. low sodium soy sauce	3 T. tamarind sauce
3 garlic cloves, minced	1 T. dry sherry
1 medium onion, chopped	1 celery rib, chopped
1 tsp. fresh thyme or 1/2 tsp. dried	1 tsp. cornstarch
1 tsp. fresh oregano or	1 T. cold water
or 1/2 tsp. dried	Salt and pepper

In a large bowl, mix the cubed meat with the soy sauce, garlic, onion, thyme, oregano, salt and pepper. Marinate for one hour.

In a large saute pan, heat the oil and brown the meat. Drain the oil from the pan and add the chicken broth, tamarind sauce, and dry sherry. Cook the meat for about 1 1/2 hours, until tender and the liquid is reduced to about 1/3. Dissolve the cornstarch in a tablespoon of cold water. Add it to the mixture, stirring until the sauce thickens.

Serve over white rice with a vegetable or a salad.

Serves: 6

FISH IN TAMARIND SAUCE
Pescado en Salsa de Tamarindo

2 lbs (or 1 kilo) fish fillets
  (sea bass or red snapper)
1/2 cup vegetable oil
6 cloves garlic, peeled, crushed,
  and minced
4 T. soy sauce

2 T. unrefined brown sugar
1/2 cup tamarind water
1 2 inch piece of fresh
  ginger, minced
6 green onions, including
  the green, cut in 1" lengths

Wash the fish fillets, trim, and dry with paper towels.

In a large frying pan, heat the oil at a high heat and fry the fillets, one at a time on both sides, until golden. Remove from the pan and drain on paper towels.

Pour out of the frying pan all but 2 tablespoons of the oil and reheat it over a medium heat. Saute the garlic until light brown. Add the soy sauce, sugar, and tamarind liquid, stirring frequently for about one minute.

Return the fish to the sauce. Sprinkle with the green onions and ginger. Heat for about 2 minutes more, spooning the sauce over the fish.

Serve topped with chopped cilantro and accompanied by white rice.

Serves: 4 to 6

OTHER TROPICAL FRUITS

There are more than 100 species of tropical fruits which serve as foods, but only about 20 are of commercial importance. These include the avocado, banana, citrus fruits, coconut, guava, mango, papaya and pineapple, all of which are cultivated in Central America for export. In the previous section, we have featured some tropical fruits found in Costa Rica which are utilized in regional cooking. To acquaint our reader with still other fruits, we list some frequently found at local markets.

Caimito: A sweet flavored fruit also known as "star apple" because of its apple size and shape. The skin is thin and smooth and deep purple in color while the flesh is white, but sometimes has purple and pink shades in the center. It should be peeled, the several black seeds removed, and eaten raw.

Chiverre: A fruit which looks just like watermelon, but has a whitish spaghetti-like pulp. The pulp is candied with *tapa dulce* (brown sugar) to make special Easter treats.

Granada: The Spanish name for the pomegranate, a tangy red fruit with many edible seeds. The peel is almost like a shell. It must be broken open to obtain the edible seeds.

Guanábana: This is a large, green-skinned fruit about the size of a papaya. The flesh is white with black seeds and is a bit acidic. It's used a good deal to make drinks, ice cream, or popsicles.

Jocote: A small fruit, no bigger than an olive with a very large seed. When ripe, it is sweet and tender while when green, it can be very acidic. It is usually eaten raw, but it can be candied.

Mamey: An oval shaped fruit with a brown pebbly skin. The flesh is reddish purple around a large seed and has a very intriguing flavor.

Mandarina: A member of the tangerine family, this pungent fruit looks like a flattened orange. The skin is dark green and easily separates from the flesh.

Manzana de Agua: Although not related to the apple, it is often called "mountain apple". Shaped like a small pear, it has red skin with white blotches. No need to peel the fruit, just eat it as you would an apple or a pear!

Melón: This term used for all types of melon-- cantaloupe, honeydew, cassaba, etc.--with the exception of watermelon *(sandia).*

Mora: The Spanish name for blackberry..they're great to use in *refrescos* and ice cream!

Nance: This small fruit has a soft and smooth yellow skin. A large round black seed is embedded in the sweet-sour pulp. The pulp is primarily used for drinks and ices.

Naranjilla: Although the name implies "little orange", it is not related to the orange. The skin is firm and smooth and varies in color from green to bright orange. The flesh is greenish-yellow and divides into sections like an orange. It contains many small seeds which must be removed before using it in natural drinks.

Níspero: About the size of a prune, it is oval-shaped and yellow skinned. The pulp is cream-colored with a tangy flavor and contains a small seed.

Zapote: A common fruit which looks like a big brown avocado. The pulp is bright red-orange and contains a large black smooth seed. The flesh is eaten raw and has a sweet flavor.

CALABAZA/AYOTE

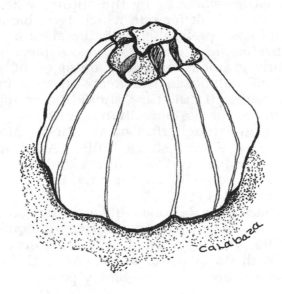

Calabaza

Calabaza is the common name for several strains of pumpkins and squashes grown in Central America and the Caribbean. Although some refer to calabaza as the West Indian Pumpkin, the calabaza is really a pumpkin-like squash. Here in Costa Rica this squash is more commonly called *ayote*.

Squashes, like beans, tomatoes, potatoes, and chilies are native to the Americas. We feature in our guide several Latin members of the squash family which are very commonly found in Central America, but relatively unknown in North America. Along with ayote, chayote and zapallo are regional produce market mainstays! With the current popularity of Southwestern and "New World" cuisine, calabaza can now be found with greater frequency in the United States, particularly in Florida. It might be featured by one of its several other names: Cuban pumpkin, Cuban squash, or even Cinderella's Coach!

Calabazas are round in shape, and their size can range from as large as a watermelon to as small as a cantaloupe. Their skin is smooth, but their color can vary from green to pale tan to light red-orange. The flesh of the calabaza is always a brilliant orange, thus the comparison to the pumpkin. Calabaza has a sweet flavor akin to that of butternut squash. Calabaza can be purchased either whole or by the chunk. When choosing whole calabazas, look for one which is unblemished and heavy for its size, preferably with the stem attached. If you are purchasing a chunk, choose a piece with fresh, moist, tightly grained flesh with no signs of soft or wet spots. Whole calabazas will keep up to a month in a cool, dark place. If cut, they should be wrapped tightly and refrigerated for no more than a week.

Slicing the tough rind of an uncut calabaza calls for a cleaver or a very sharp knife. After opening the squash, remove the seed and fibers and proceed as you would with any squash. By the way, the crisp seeds are delicious toasted!

Calabaza may be used in any way suitable to its close cousins, the acorn and butternut squashes. The flesh may be simply steamed or baked, serving it as a vegetable. With its delicate, sweet flavor, the calabaza is great for soups, breads, and holiday pies.

CALABAZA PUREE
Puré de Ayote

3 1/2 lbs. calabaza, peeled, seeded, and cut into 2-inch chunks
1/4 cup extra-virgin olive oil
2 to 3 T fresh lime juice, or to taste
freshly grated nutmeg to taste

In a steamer set over boiling water, steam the squash, covered, for 15 to 20 minutes, or until it is very tender. Reserve the steaming liquid and force the squash through a ricer or a food mill set over a large bowl. Stir in the oil, the lime juice, and enough of the reserved steaming liquid to reach the desired consistency. Season the squash puree with nutmeg and salt and pepper.

The puree may be made 3 days in advance, kept covered and chilled, and reheated, adding additional water as needed. Serve as a part of a holiday buffet.

Makes: about 6 cups

HOLIDAY CALABAZA SOUP
Sopa de Ayote para Fiestas

1 1/2 to 1 3/4 lb. piece calabaza
2 T. unsalted butter
1 onion, diced
1 carrot, diced
2 ribs celery, diced
3 cloves garlic, diced
2 jalapeño chilies, seeded and
   diced (optional)

4 to 5 cups chicken stock
2 bay leaves
2 sprigs fresh thyme or 1 tsp.
   dried thyme
1/4 cup finely chopped fresh
   Italian (flat leaf) parsley
Salt and pepper to taste
1/2 cup half and half, light
   cream or whipping cream

Spice-scented Whipped Cream and Garnish:
1/2 cup whipping cream
1/4 tsp. ground cumin
1/4 tsp. ground coriander

1/4 tsp. cayenne pepper
Salt and pepper to taste
1 T. finely chopped fresh
   chives or scallions

Using a sharp knife, cut the rind off the calabaza. Scrape out any seeds with a spoon and cut the flesh into 1-inch pieces.

Melt the butter in a large saucepan over medium heat. Saute the onion, carrot, and celery until soft but not brown, 3 to 4 minutes. Add the garlic and chilies and cook for 1 minute.

Stir in the calabaza, 4 cups of the stock, the herbs, and seasonings and bring to a boil. Reduce the heat and simmer the soup, uncovered, until the vegetables are very soft, about 30 minutes. Remove the bay leaves and thyme branches, and puree the soup in a blender.

Return the soup to the saucepan and stir in the cream. If the soup is too thick, add more stock. Correct the seasonings, adding salt or pepper.

Prepare the spice-scented whipped cream: Beat the cream to soft peaks in a chilled bowl. Whip in the spices and salt and pepper.

To serve, ladle the soup into bowls and place a dollop of the cream with the chives and serve at once.

Serves: 6

CHAYOTE

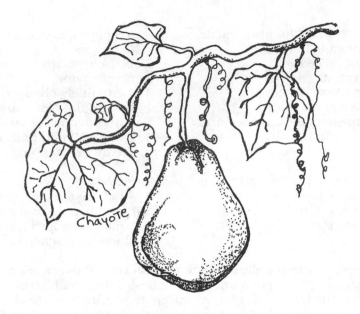

chayote

Chayote, *sechium edule*, is a squash-like vegetable, native to Central America and Southern Mexico. It was once the principal food of the Aztecs and Mayans and remains a very popular vegetable in this region today. Sometimes referred to as the "vegetable pear", the chayote is usually about the size and shape of a large pear or avocado.

Depending on the variety, the chayote's thin skin, laced with small furrows, is light green, dark green, or off-white. The tuberous flesh is white, containing a single soft seed. Both green and white chayotes are available in Costa Rica. A very small white variety, *chayote cocoro*, also can be found.

Chayotes grow on vines and require little care. *Campesinos* (farmers) say the vine should be planted by your house because chayotes like people! A single plant with no nurturing can provide up to a 1000 fruits a year. Their abundance makes the chayote Costa Rica's most popular vegetable.

Chayotes have a rather bland-tasting flesh which usually requires decided seasoning to suit most palettes. The chayote seed is edible as is the skin. Chayotes can

can be prepared in any manner suitable for summer squash-- baked, boiled, steamed, or sauteed. Since chayotes are very firm (members of the gourd family) they always must be cooked before eating.

To boil the chayote, first peel it, then chop it into cubed pieces, rinse off the sticky juice, and boil it in water for about 45 minutes. The chayote is used in picadillos, stews, and numerous entrees. Additionally, it is added to salads, mashed like a potato, batter fried like zucchini, and stuffed like eggplant! By themselves chayotes are low in calories, but they are frequently served in sauces utilizing butter and cream.

The "rule of thumb" when choosing a chayote is: "the harder, the better". Chayotes will keep for 2 to 3 weeks in the refrigerator.

CORN AND CHAYOTE SOUP
Sopa de Elote y Chayote

2-3 large ears of corn, or 2 cups canned or
   frozen
2 large green onions chopped
2 T. butter
1/3 cup diced carrot
1 large celery stalk, chopped
3 cups chicken broth
1 garlic clove, minced
1/2 cup chayote, cubed and cooked

Salsa Fresca:

2 small tomatoes (1/2 lb.),
   peeled and chopped
1 jalapeño pepper, seeded
   and chopped

1/4 cup cilantro, chopped
1/3 cup onion, chopped
1/4 tsp. salt

Mix all the ingredients together in a bowl at room temperature.

If using fresh corn, cut about 2 cups kernels from the cobs. Melt the butter in a large sauce pan. Add the corn, celery, garlic, and onions. Saute for 10 minutes. Add the carrots and broth, and salt to taste. After bringing to a boil, reduce the heat, cover, and simmer gently for 45 minutes. Finally, add the cooked chayote and heat thoroughly.

Served topped with the *salsa fresca*.

Serves: 6

105

MARINATED VEGETABLES
Escabeche

1 cauliflower, cut into florets	6 bay leaves
1 chayote, juliened	1 T. prepared mustard, Dijon
1/2 lb. green beans, juliened	1/2 cup white wine vinegar
1/2 lb. carrots, juliened	1/4 cup olive oil
1 medium onion, cut into rings	4 garlic cloves, minced
1 green bell pepper, juliened	Salt and pepper to taste

Cut the first four ingredients--cauliflower, chayote, green beans and carrots--Blanche in hot water for a few minutes, removing the vegetables from the water while still crisp.

Heat the oil and saute the onion, minced garlic, and bell peppers along with the bay leaves for about 2 minutes, until transparent, but not limp.

Mix both mixtures together, and add salt and pepper to taste. Add the vinegar mixed with the mustard. Cool, then refrigerate.

Serves: 6 to 8

STUFFED CHAYOTE
Chancletas

5 medium white chayotes	1/4 cup finely chopped celery
6 oz. Jack or Turrialba cheese	4 T. chopped parsley
1/2 cup bread crumbs	1/4 cup Parmesan cheese
3 T. cream	

Place the whole chayotes in a saucepan, cover with water, and bring to a boil. Reduce the heat and simmer for about 30 to 45 minutes, until fork tender. Remove, cool, and slice lengthwise in half without tearing the shells, then remove the pulp.

Mix the cheeses, celery, and parsley. Mash the pulp and add to the mixture. Stir in the cream. Fill the shells with the mixture, sprinkling the top of each with bread crumbs. Bake at 350°F for 15 minutes.

Serves: 10

CHAYOTE AND CORN HASH
Picadillo de Chayote y Elote

1 medium onion, chopped
1 bell pepper, chopped
4 young chayotes, peeled
   and cubed
l bunch cilantro, chopped
2 celery stalks, minced
1 lb. ground beef
2 T. cooking oil
2 T. Salsa Lizano or Lea-Perrins
   Sauce

2 cloves garlic, minced
1 cube beef boullion
1/2 tsp. black pepper
1 tsp. cumin
1 tsp. ground coriander
1 1/2 cups corn, fresh or
   canned
1 medium tomato, chopped
1 cup water

Mix the meat with the Lizano sauce, garlic, pepper, cumin, and ground coriander. Set aside. Fry the onion, bell pepper, celery, and chopped cilantro in 2 tablespoons cooking oil. When the onion is tender and transparent, add the chopped tomato and the meat mixture. Cook at medium heat for about 5 minutes. Add the cubed chayote, cover and cook for about 20 minutes or until the chayote is tender. Stir frequently so the mixture does not dry, adding water as needed. Add the corn and cook for another 10 minutes.

Serves: 6 to 8

CILANTRO/CULANTRO

Although cilantro, *culantro* in Spanish, is technically an herb, we include it amongst our tropical vegetables because of its widespread use in Latin cuisine. This annual herb, *coriandrum sativum*, is a member of the parsley family and is also known as coriander and Chinese parsley. In addition to its use in Latin American and Caribbean cooking, cilantro is a basic flavoring ingredient in many Oriental dishes. Interestingly, this herb is native to southern Europe and has been transported to Asia and Latin America!

Cilantro looks like a light green parsley. The leaves are more fern-like and delicate with a "soapy" texture. With a spicy perfume, the flavor of cilantro is quite distinctive. As a seasoning, people seem to love cilantro or hate it...but cilantro has a way of growing on you. More and more frequently when we want flavoring, especially to spice up dishes, we use cilantro in place of parsley.

Cilantro is cheap and readily available throughout Central America the year around. It is sold, like parsley, in small bunches. To select for freshness, look for cilantro bunches with bright green leaves, even in color. The leaves should show no sign of wilting and be free from browning and decay.

Cilantro is highly perishable, so to store it take the bunch apart and place the unwashed leaves in a plastic bag. Cilantro can also be stored by placing the bunch, stems down, in a glass of water and covering it with a plastic bag, secured to the container with a rubber band. To prevent spoilage, cilantro should not be washed until just prior to using. Always refrigerate cilantro and always use it as soon as possible! Just before using cilantro, wash it and pat it dry with paper towels.

Both the leaves and the seeds of the cilantro plant may be used in cooking. The seeds, usually called coriander seeds, can be crushed and added to stews and pastries. The are also used to season sausages, bean and stew dishes, and even cookies and wines! The cilantro plant's aromatic oil is used in beverages, candles, tobacco, and perfumes. We are most concerned here with the cilantro leaves. They have a variety of uses in salads, sauces, soups, curries, and meat, poultry, and fish dishes!

Cilantro is most definitely a very useful herb!

HOT TIPS!

- Use cilantro as you would parsley.
- Garnish soups with cilantro.
- Chop cilantro and add it to dips.
- Sprinkle it over fresh fish.
- Add it to pasta and bean dishes.

TOMATO RELISH
Chirimol

5 medium sized ripe tomatoes
   peeled, seeded, and chopped
1 medium sized onion
1/3 cup finely chopped green bell pepper

2 T. chopped fresh cilantro
1 T. finely chopped fresh mint
Salt and pepper to taste

Combine all the ingredients in a bowl and refrigerate. The sauce will keep up to two days. Serve it with grilled meats or chicken or use as a dip with tortilla chips.

Makes: 2 cups

CILANTRO PESTO
Pesto de Culantro

2 cups fresh cilantro
3 cloves garlic minced
1 T. fresh lime juice

1/4 cup olive oil
1/2 tsp. salt
1/2 tsp. fresh ground pepper

Place the cilantro leaves and garlic in the food processor or blender. With the motor running, slowly drizzle in the lime juice and oil, blending until the cilantro is pureed.

Transfer the pesto to a bowl and stir in the salt and pepper. Refrigerate, covered, until ready to use. It will keep in the refrigerator for 2 days.

The pesto can be used to flavor pasta or baked potatoes. It can be dabbed atop black bean nachos, spooned into guacamole, or spread on chicken fajitas. Perhaps you can invent other uses for it!

Makes: 1/2 cup

CILANTRO SLAW
Ensalada de Culantro y Repollo

1 head green cabbage (about 1lb.),
   finely shredded
1 small onion, minced
Salt and pepper to taste

2 cucumbers, seeded and
   grated
4 T. minced fresh cilantro

* *Lime-Garlic Dressing:* Mix 1/2 cup salad oil with 1/2 cup lime juice, and add 2 minced cloves of garlic. Shake in a jar to mix well.

Mix the cabbage, onion, and cilantro in a large bowl. Peel and seed the cucumber. Stir the Lime-Garllic dressing into the cabbage. Garnish with cucumber. Season to taste with salt and pepper.

Serves: 6 to 8

CILANTRO AND CORN SOUFFLE
Souffle de Culantro y Elote

2 cups corn kernels, fresh
   or canned
1 cup grated cheddar cheese
1/2 stick butter in pieces
6 egg yolks
salt and pepper

1/2 cup corn, drained
3 tomatoes, peeled and finely
   chopped
5 T. chopped cilantro
6 egg whites

Put 2 cups corn, cheddar cheese, and butter in a blender. With the machine running, add the egg yolks, one at a time. Then, put this mixture into a mixing bowl and add tomatoes, cilantro, and 1/2 cup of corn, drained if canned.   Salt and pepper to taste.

Beat the egg whites until dry, but not stiff. Add a pinch of salt, and fold the egg whites into the mixture.

Grease a souffle dish and pour in the batter. Bake in a preheated 350°F oven for about 30 minutes, until golden. Opening the oven door during baking will cause the souffle to fall.

Serves: 4 to 6

CAJUN FRIED CALAMARI WITH CILANTRO-LIME DIP
Calamares Fritos con Dip de Culantro y Limón

2 lbs. calamari, cleaned
1 1/2 cups all-purpose flour
1/4 cup ground cumin
1/4 cup chili powder
1 cup Creamy Lime Dressing (p.52)
1/4 cup chopped cilantro

1 tsp. coarse black pepper
1/2 tsp. salt
2 cups corn oil
Tabasco sauce, to taste

Rinse the calamari, cut them into 1/4 inch thick rings, and lay on paper towels to dry.

Combine the flour, cumin, chili powder, pepper, and salt in a shallow bowl or dish.

Heat the oil in a large skillet. When it is very hot, dredge the calamari in the flour mixture, shake off any excess, and fry in the oil (in several batches) until brown and crispy.   As the calamari are frying, sprinkle several dashes of Tabasco on them, depending on how spicy you want them to be. Drain on paper towels.

Stir the cilantro into the lime dressing and use it as a dip for the calamari.

Serves: 4

COSTA RICAN COUNTRY HASH
Picadillo Campesino Costarricense

3 lbs. peeled potatoes
1 lb. beef, any cut good for
   shredding (stewing beef)
1 tsp. Salsa Lizano
1 bunch of cilantro, chopped
1 rib celery, chopped
1 green pepper, chopped
1 medium onion, chopped

3 minced garlic cloves
1 tomato, pureed in a cup
   of water
1 cup water
1/4 tsp. oregano
1/4 tsp. ground black pepper
1/4 tsp. achiote paste
Fresh tortillas

Cook the meat with the pureed tomato, cup of water, onions, pepper, garlic, celery, and all the spices, except the achiote paste. Bring to a boil, reduce heat, cover, and simmer for 1 hour or until meat is tender. If using a pressure cooker, cook for 20 minutes.

When the meat is done, remove it from the liquid. Add the whole potatoes to the liquid and cook until tender. As the potatoes cook, if more liquid is needed, add a small amount of water.

Meanwhile shred the meat using two forks. When the potatoes are cooked, remove and cube them. Add the cubed potatoes to the shredded meat along with 1 cup of the cooking liquid. Add the achiote paste and salt and pepper to taste.

To be *muy tipico*, serve this dish with fresh tortillas.
Serves: 6 to 8

GREEN ONION/CEBOLLIN

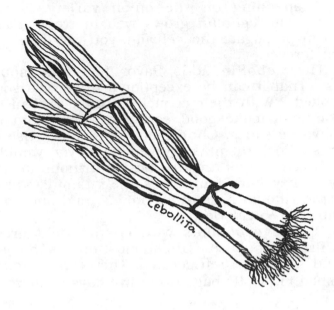

No cook can function without onions!! There are hundreds of varieties, and they can be sauteed, boiled, steamed, braised, baked, or eaten raw! The yellow onion makes up 75 percent of the world's supply and is the most readily available onion in Costa Rica. Since the yellow onion, *cebolla seca*, can be pungent, it is most often cooked. Those found in Central America are a little milder than their Stateside cousins and could be eaten raw, but we prefer the red or purple onion, *cebolla morada*. It's delicious sweetness is perfect for salads and sandwiches; the only problem is they are a bit hard to locate. Purple onions, however, can always be found at roadside stands in Santa Ana, Costa Rica's onion capital, but one has to spend time looking for them in San José and other locales. White onions, sold in bunches with the green stem and a fairly good size bulb in comparison to their northern counterparts, are also frequently found.

We list the green onion, *cebollín*, in our guide because it is often overlooked. The green onion, *allium sepa*, is basically a baby or immature onion with a thin bulb and green top. It's usually sold in bunches and has a myriad of English names from scallion to spring onion

113

to green bunching onion. It can be sweetly mild or a bit biting, depending on the onion variety to which it belongs. The *cebollín* grows well in tropical climates. Once you propagate the *cebollín*, you will have it in your garden forever.

The *cebollín* adds flavor to stews, soups and salads. That it can be exceptional braised is sometimes overlooked. With their crunchy texture and nice flavor, these onions make good eating raw, just dip them in your favorite sauce. Chop them for salads. Use them in stir-fries. Cook them as a vegetable as you would leeks.

Green onions are the most nutritious in the onion family. They have four times the vitamin C and 5,000 times the vitamin A as other onions, and one pound has only about 175 calories!

Choose *cebollines* with crisp, bright green tops and a firm white base. Unlike most onions, green onions can and should be refrigerated. They can be refrigerated unwashed in plastic bags up to five days or more.

BRAISED SCALLIONS IN MUSTARD SAUCE
Cebollines con Salsa Mostaza

20 to 24 scallions (green onions)	2 parsley sprigs
1 T. sweet butter	fresh black pepper, to taste
1 celery rib, chopped	1 1/2 cups chicken broth
1 carrot, peeled and chopped	1/4 cup Dijon-style mustard
1 tsp. dried thyme	1/2 cup heavy cream
1 bay leaf	salt (optional)

Trim and clean the scallions and cut away all but about 2 inches of the green tops. Save tops for another use if you like.

In a skillet large enough to hold the scallions later, melt the butter and cook the celery and carrot over low heat, covered, until tender and lightly colored about 20 minutes.

Add the thyme, bay leaf, parsley, black pepper to taste, and chicken broth. Simmer together, partially covered, for 15 minutes. Add no salt at this point; you will correct seasoning as necessary when the dish is completed.

Add the scallions to the broth and simmer, uncovered. for about 5 minutes, until barely tender. Do not overcook. Remove scallions with a slotted spoon and reserve.

Strain the liquid, discard the solids, measure out 1/2 cup, and return it to the skillet. Whisk in the mustard and the heavy cream. Set the skillet over medium heat and simmer, stirring occasionally, for 10 minutes, or until sauce is reduced by about one third. Taste and correct seasoning.

Return scallions to the skillet for 1 minute to warm them through before serving. The braised scallions are rich and aromatic, thus are best served with roasted or barbecued meats.

Serves: 4 to 6

PAN-FRIED FISH WITH SCALLIONS
Pescado Frito con Cebollines

18 green onions (scallions), white bulbs and 5 inches of the green (Try to buy fresh ones with small, thin bulbs!)

6 white fish fillets, about 2 pounds

1/2 cup olive oil	1 cup all-purpose flour
1 tsp. course ground black pepper	1/2 tsp. cayenne pepper
1 tsp. dried thyme leaves	Salt and pepper to taste
1 T. chopped fresh parsley	1 cup (2 sticks) unsalted
1 cup milk	butter, clarified
1 cup yellow cornmeal	2 T. chopped cilantro

Heat the olive oil in a large skillet over medium heat. Add the scallions, and cook, turning them with tongs, until just wilted, 2 minutes. Sprinkle them with the pepper and thyme as they cook. Remove the scallions from the skillet, sprinkle them with the parsley, and set aside.

Pour the milk into a glass pie plate. Mix the cornmeal, flour, cayenne, and salt and pepper together in a second pie plate. Dip the fish fillets first in the milk, then in the cornmeal mixture.

Melt the butter in a large skillet over medium heat. Saute the fish until golden on both sides, 3 minutes per side.

Place the fish on a serving platter, and garnish each fillet with three scallions. Sprinkle with the chopped cilantro. It's tasty served with roasted sweet peppers and black beans.

Serves: 6

ACAPULCO ENCHILADA
Enchilada de Acapulco

3 cups shredded poached chicken
  breasts
1/2 cup minced green onions
  (white and some of green part)
1/2 cup chopped blanched almonds
1/2 tsp. salt
Additional sour cream and green
  green onions to serve on the side

8 flat corn tortillas (must
  be very fresh)
3/4 cup sour cream
1/2 cup shredded Cheddar
  cheese
1/2 cup sliced pitted black
  olives

3 cups **Enchilada Chili Sauce** (Ingredients follow)

2 T. vegetable oil
3/4 cup chopped onion
1/4 cup chopped green bell pepper
1 garlic clove, minced
1 cup tomato paste

1 cup water
1/4 cup chili powder
1 tsp. salt
1/2 tsp. dried oregano

In a small bowl, toss together the shredded chicken, scallions, and almonds. Sprinkle on the salt, mix, and set aside.

To prepare the chili sauce heat the oil in a sauté pan over medium-high heat; add the onion, bell pepper, and garlic and saute until the vegetables are soft. Stir in the tomato paste, water, chili powder, salt, and oregano, blending well. Lower the heat, cover, and simmer for 5 minutes.

Preheat the oven to 350°F.

To assemble the enchiladas, lightly oil the bottom of a shallow oven proof casserole. Dip a tortilla in the hot sauce until partially saturated. Then place the tortilla in the casserole dish; fill with one eighth of the chicken mixture, and top with 1 tablespoon of sour cream; roll into an enchilada, seam side down. Repeat with the remaining tortillas. When the casserole is filled, drizzle the remaining sauces over the enchiladas, sprinkle with Cheddar cheese, and top with olives.

Bake the enchiladas for 15 minutes, or until the cheese and sauce are hot and bubbling. Serve with additional sour cream and chopped green onion on the side.

Serves: 4

HEARTS OF PALM/PALMITO

Palmito Palm

One of the delights of living in Central America is the availability of hearts of palm, *palmito* in Spanish. Up north hearts of palm can rarely be found fresh, although they can be found in cans and jars. Additionally, they are so costly most purchase hearts of palm only for special occasions! Here in Costa Rica, you can purchase fresh *palmito* the year around...and it is reasonable. If one does not want to go to the trouble of cooking *palmito*, processed hearts of palm are available at supermarkets.

Hearts of palm are the edible inner portion of the stem of the cabbage palm tree, a tree which grows in many tropical climes. The vegetable has also been called "swamp cabbage", a name which would endear it to few, palm cabbage, and palmettos.

The thought of hearts of palm makes most epicure's mouths water! They are tropical delicacies which not only enhance salads and main dishes, but are savored by themselves as appetizers. Each stalk is about 4 inches long and can range in diameter from pencil-thin to about 1 1/2 inches. Slender and ivory-colored, hearts of palm resemble white asparagus, sans tips, and are utilized in a similar fashion. Their texture is firm and smooth and the flavor is reminiscent of an artichoke heart.

Although much easier to use, canned hearts of palm tend to be mushier than fresh ones and are loaded with sodium as a preservative. Once cans are open, the contents should be transferred to an airtight nonmetal container. They can be refrigerated in their liquid a couple of weeks or more.

TO PREPARE

To prepare fresh palmito...
Cover the cylindrical pieces with water and let them soak for an hour. Blanche them for about 5 minutes. Drain and put into fresh water. Bring to a boil and cook covered until tender, about 45 minutes.

SUNSHINE SALAD
Ensalada del Sol

1/2 cup fresh orange juice
1/4 cup fresh lime juice
3 T. extra-virgin olive oil
1 1/2 T. honey
1 T. balsamic vinegar
1 1/2 tsp. Dijon mustard
1 1/2 tsp. pink peppercorns,
   lightly crushed with side of a knife

1 tsp. finely chopped fresh tarragon
Plenty of salt and black pepper
2 cups thinly sliced hearts of palm,
   fresh or drained canned
4 to 5 cups mixed baby salad greens
1 T. finely chopped fresh chives

Combine the ingredients for the marinade in a nonreactive mixing bowl and whisk until smooth. Add the hearts of palm. If using fresh hearts of palm, marinate for 4 hours. If using canned hearts of palm, marinate for 1 hour. Place a saucer over the hearts of palm to keep them submerged.

Drain the hearts of palm, reserving the marinade. Toss the salad greens with 3 to 4 tablespoons of marinade and arrange on the salad plates. Arrange the palm hearts on top. Spoon a little more marinade over the palm hearts and sprinkle with finely chopped chives.

Serves: 4 to 6

POTATO SALAD WITH HEARTS OF PALM
Ensalada de Papas con Palmito

1 lb. potatoes, cooked, peeled, and cubed
1 8 oz. can Hearts of Palm, cut into rounds
1/2 T. Worcestershire sauce

1 medium onion, minced
2 hard boiled eggs, cubed
3 T. fresh parsley, chopped
Salt and pepper to taste
1 cup mayonnaise, approx.

Mix in a small bowl the mayonnaise, onion, and Worcestershire sauce. Salt and pepper to taste. In a larger bowl, mix the cooled cubed potatoes with the palmito and the egg. Add the mayonnaise mixture, and mix well. Refrigerate. When serving, sprinkle the chopped parsley on top.
Serves: 4 to 6

RICE AND HEARTS OF PALM CASSEROLE
Cacerola de Arroz y Palmito

4 to 6 cups cooked white rice
2 cups grated mozzarella or Monterey Jack cheese

1 can Hearts of Palm

White Sauce:
1/2 stick butter or margarine
1/2 cup onion, minced
1/2 green bell pepper, minced
4 cups of milk

3 T. flour
2 chicken boullion cubes
Salt and pepper to taste

Grease an oven-proof 9 x 13 pyrex dish. Put one layer of rice on the bottom topped with a layer of palmito, then add a layer of white sauce. Repeat the layering, finishing with a layer of rice. Cover the top of the casserole with the grated cheese.
Cover the top with aluminum foil and bake at 300°F for about 30 minutes. Remove the foil for the last 10 minutes of cooking so the cheese will melt and slightly brown.
Serves: 8

White Sauce:
Sauté the onions and bell pepper in melted butter or margarine. Add 3 cups of milk, the bullion cubes, and salt and pepper to taste. In a small mixing bowl, mix the flour and the remaining cup of milk. Add it to the mixture, and boil until thickened.

HEARTS OF PALM AU GRATIN
Palmito al Gratin

1 cup evaporated milk
1 cup milk
5 T. butter
2 T. minced onion
2 T. cornstarch, dissolved in
    1/4 cup chicken broth
1/2 cup bread crumbs

pinch of nutmeg
salt and pepper to taste
1/4 cup parmesan cheese
2 egg yolks
2 lbs. cooked hearts of palm,
    sliced (or two cans)

Put the evaporated milk, milk, cornstarch, nutmeg, salt and pepper into the blender and mix. In a medium sauce pan melt 2 tablespoons butter and saute the onion. Add the milk mixture to the sauce pan, stirring constantly until thickened.

Remove the sauce pan from the heat and add the egg yolks and the parmesan cheese, stirring with a wire whisk. Return to a low heat and add the hearts of palm.

Pour the mixture into a greased 9-inch square or round pyrex baking dish. Sprinkle the top with parmesan cheese and the bread crumbs. Dot it with the remaining 3 tablespoons butter.

Bake at 325°F. for 15 to 20 minutes.
Serves: 6 to 8

SWEET PEPPER/CHILE DULCE

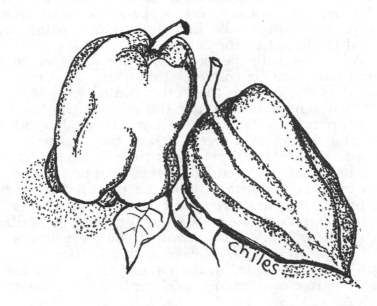

The chile pepper is another vegetable native to the tropical areas of the Americas. The term "sweet pepper", *chile dulce* in Spanish, embraces a variety of mild peppers belonging to the *Capsicum* family. Chile peppers differ in flavor and in heat intensity depending on their type. Fiery red peppers like the *habanero* (Scotch Bonnet), the *jalapeño* and the *serrano* have long been associated with Latin cooking, however, they are difficult to find in Costa Rica, thus are seldom used locally.

Both sweet and hot peppers were introduced to Europe by Christopher Columbus who brought them back to Spain where they were quickly incorporated into Spanish cuisine. The Spanish are also responsible for their introduction into North American cuisine where in recent years peppers have gained much popularity.

We give attention to sweet peppers rather than their hot brethren because Central Americans widely use them in just about everything! Sweet peppers can range in color from pale to dark green, from yellow to orange to red, and even from purple to brown and black. Their color can be solid or variegated. Most typically, green, red, or variegated peppers are found in Costa Rica. The local sweet peppers differ from "bell peppers", the best known sweet pepper in North America. Bell peppers are so named because of their bell-like shape and flat bottom. Local sweet peppers are heart-shaped with a pointed bottom and are more akin to what would be called pimientos in the States.

When choosing peppers, look for ones which are firm and have a richly colored, shiny skin. As a rule, the heavier it is for its size, the better the pepper. Another rule is: in general, the larger the pepper, the milder it is. Peppers can be stored in a plastic bag in the refrigerator for up to a week. Once they become limp, shriveled or have soft spots, it's time to discard them! For some unknown reason, green peppers seem to remain fresh and crisp a little longer than red peppers.

Sweet peppers are used raw in salads or on vegetable platters. When cooking, they can be sauteed, baked, grilled, braised or steamed. Sweet peppers are used to season soups, stews, and stir-fries. Finely chopped, they are added to salsas and dips. They are an excellent source of vitamin C and contain fair amounts of vitamin A.

A little known fact is the heat of peppers is concentrated in the interior veins or ribs near the seed heart, not in the seeds themselves. Thus, to decrease the heat intensity of any pepper, it is critical to remove the ribs as well as the seeds. If it is a hot pepper, it's best to wear gloves to protect the hands and face.

HOT TIP!

To Quick Roast and Peel Peppers...

Bake in a hot oven, char over an open flame, or broil, turning frequently, until the skin is blackened. Then place the peppers in a plastic bag and let them sweat until cool enough to handle. The skin will easily peel off.

Roasted peppers can be spooned over bread or used as a topping for grilled fish and roast chicken, risotto, polenta, crisp flat breads or pizzas. They may be tucked into sandwiches, tortillas, tacos...and more!

RED PEPPER AND GINGER RELISH
Condimento de Chile Dulce y Jengibre

12 red bell peppers (about 3 lbs.)
4 T. unsalted butter (1 stick)
1/2 cup extra virgin olive oil
3 rounded T. minced garlic
   (about 10 cloves)

Grated zest of 3 oranges
3/4 cup orange juice
3 T. sugar
2 T. fresh black pepper
1/2 cup coarsely grated fresh
   ginger

Core and seed the peppers, and cut them into 1/4-inch wide lengthwise strips. You should have 12 cups.

Heat the butter and oil in a heavy flameproof casserole. Add the garlic and ginger, and cook over low heat for 5 minutes. Add the peppers, and stir well to coat.

Mix the orange zest, juice, sugar, and pepper. Stir gently and cover. Cook over medium-low heat, stirring occasionally, until the peppers are wilted and their skins are soft, 25 minutes. Remove the cover and continue cooking over low heat, stirring frequently, until most of the liquid has evaporated, about 2 hours.

Serve hot or at room temperature. This keeps, covered tightly, in the refrigerator for up to 4 days. This recipe creates a slightly sweet condiment with a bite to it. It's great served with grilled chicken or beef, sausages, lamb, or on a sandwich or in a potato!

Makes: 4 cups

COLD SPANISH SOUP
Gazpacho

6 large ripe tomatoes
2 red peppers
2 medium yellow onions
2 large shallots, or white part
   of green onions
2 cucumbers
1/2 cup red wine vinegar

1/2 cup olive oil
1 1/2 cups canned tomato
   juice
1/2 cup chopped fresh dill
pinch of cayenne pepper
salt and pepper to taste

Garnishes: croutons, chopped hard boiled egg, chopped green onion tops, chopped cilantro, chopped red onion, chopped cucumber, and a host of other items can be used. Use your imagination and choose whatever you would like!

Wash and prepare the vegetables. Core and coarsely chop the tomatoes, saving the juice. Core, seed, and coarsely chop the peppers. Peel and coarsely chop the onions and shallots. Peel, seed, and coarsely chop the cucumbers.

In a bowl whisk together vinegar, olive oil, reserved tomato juice and canned tomato juice.

In a blender or a food processor fitted with a steel blade, puree the vegetables in small batches, adding the tomato-juice mixture as necessary to keep the blades from clogging. Do not puree completely. The gazpacho should retain some of its crunch.

Stir in cayenne, salt and pepper to taste, and dill. Cover and chill for at least 4 hours. To serve, stir, taste and correct seasoning, and ladle into chilled soup bowls or mugs. Serve with small bowls containing a number of garnishes.

Serves: 8 to 10

PICKLED FISH
Escabeche de Pescado

2 cups unbleached, all- purpose
   flour
4 lbs. fish steaks or fillets,
   1/2 inch thick
1 1/2 cups quality olive oil
juice of 1 1/2 limes
2/3 cup white wine vinegar
2/3 cup dry white wine
2 2/3 cups green beans, julienne
1 1/3 cups carrots, julienne
1/3 cup green pitted olives,
   with juice
1/2 cup black pitted olives,
   without juice
1/3 cup capers
1 1/2 T. brown sugar
3 garlic cloves, finely chopped

1 medium purple onion, cut
   into thin rounds
1 small white onion, cut
   into thin rounds
2 green peppers, cut into
   thin rings
2 red peppers, cut into
   thin rings
1 T. Oriental oyster sauce
3 T. fresh cilantro, coarsely
   chopped
3 T. fresh dill, coarsely
   chopped
1 T. mixed pickling spice
1 tsp. salt
Fresh black pepper to taste

Flour the fish lightly. Heat the oil in a large skillet and saute the fish, in batches if necessary, for 3 to 4 minutes, turning frequently. Fish should be just cooked and starting to brown lightly. Remove from skillet and drain on paper towels.

Transfer drained fish to a large bowl. Combine all liquids and seasonings, mix with vegetables, and pour over fish. Cover and refrigerate for 4 days, basting at intervals.

Toss again, arrange on a large platter, and garnish with additional chopped parsley. Serve immediately.

This escabeche will keep refrigerated for 2 weeks. It can be made with any firm-fleshed white fish. Serve it with fresh bread and white rice. It's a great outdoor meal!

Makes: 12 to 14 portions

"PURA VIDA" CHICKEN
Pollo Pura Vida

8 chicken legs and thighs

8 green bell peppers, roasted, peeled, and cut in lengths

6 large potatoes, peeled, cut in fourths, and cooked

2 chicken boullion cubes, dissolved in 2 cups hot water

2 medium onions, sliced

2 cups whipping cream or milk

3 T. vegetable oil

Salt and pepper to taste

In a very large frying or sauté pan, brown both sides of the chicken in the hot oil. Add the onion, sauting until translucent. Add salt, pepper, and the water with the dissolved chicken boullion cubes. Cover and cook about 20 minutes.

Finally, add the potato chunks, bell pepper lengths, and the cream. Simmer for 10 to 15 minutes, until everything is thoroughly heated.

Serve with rice and a green salad.

Serves: 8

SWEET POTATO/CAMOTE

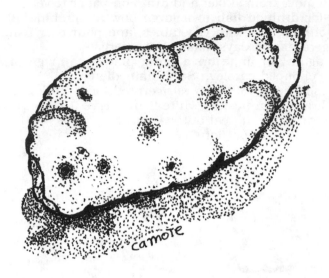

camote

This edible root is native to the tropical areas of the Americas. One of the earliest domesticated plants, there is evidence the sweet potato was cultivated in southern Peru and Mexico more than 4000 years before Christ. In the 16th century Portuguese explorers carried the sweet potato to Africa, India, and Southeast Asia. In Europe, the sweet potato's commercial value was no doubt enhanced when it gained a reputation as an aphrodisiac!

There are many varieties of the sweet potato of which the *camote* is just one. This variety is very common in Central America and the Caribbean, and is often referred to as the tropical sweet potato or the Cuban sweet potato. Other Spanish names in these regions are *boniato* and *batata* after its botanical name, *ipomoea batata*. The camote is a turnip-shaped, elongated and bumpy root with patchy reddish brown skin. It has a paler yellow flesh than some sweet potato varieties. (Darker sweet potato varieties with a more vivid orange flesh are often erroneously call "yams", a species not related to the sweet potato.)

Camotes can be baked, boiled, fried, canned, frozen, or even "microwaved" like a potato! When selecting camotes, make sure you choose ones which are firm and without bruises. While the root has some moisture uncooked, after cooking it looses its moisture and becomes fairly dry and flaky. Like other tubers, camotes should not be stored in the refrigerator and are best kept in a cool, dark place for no more than a week before using.

Since they have such a sweet chestnut-like flavor, we like camotes simply baked like a potato. Peeled camotes can be boiled and used in casseroles, pies, cookies and other desserts or just served pureed. As a result of deep frying, camotes also make great "chips" and "french fried" potatoes.

VELVETY SWEET POTATO SOUP
Sopa de Terciopelo

4 T. (1 stick) unsalted butter	6 cups chicken stock/ broth
4 cups canned pumpkin	1 tsp. fresh black pepper
(or fresh butter nut squash)	1 tsp. salt
2 cups cooked and pureed sweet	Sour cream, for garnish
potatoes (camote)	Snipped fresh chives,
1 cup smooth peanut butter	for garnish

Melt the butter in a soup pot over a medium heat. Stir in the pumpkin, sweet potatoes, and peanut butter.

Add the stock, pepper, and salt, and stir well until smooth. Reduce the heat to a simmer and cook for 20 minutes.

Before serving, garnish the soup with chives and sour cream.

This soup is a winner, so don't turn up your nose before trying it!

Serves: 8

SWEET POTATO PANCAKES
Panqué de Camote

2 cups mashed cooked sweet	1/2 tsp. fresh ground pepper
potato	1/2 tsp. salt
2 eggs, lightly beaten	1/4 tsp. cayenne pepper
1/2 cup coarsely grated onion	8 T. (1 stick) unsalted butter
4 T. unbleached all-purpose flour	4 T. (1/4 cup) solid vegetable
1 tsp. grated nutmeg	shortening
1 tsp. curry powder	chunky applesauce, cold

Combine the potatoes and eggs in a medium size mixing bowl. Put the grated onion in the center of a clean kitchen towel, wring the liquid out of it. Add the onion to the bowl.

Add the flour, nutmeg, curry powder, black pepper, salt, and cayenne; stir well. Cover with plastic wrap and refrigerate for 1 hour.

Heat 2 tablespoons of the butter and 1 tablespoon of the shortening in a medium-size non stick skillet over medium heat. Form the potato mixture into patties and add them to the hot skillet, three at a time. Spread them out to form pancakes 1/4 inch thick and 3 inches in diameter. Brown them on one side, then turn and cook until the other side is golden brown. Arrange the cooked pancakes on a paper towel lined baking sheet, and keep them warm in the oven.

Repeat until all the potato mixture is used up, adding more butter and shortening as necessary. Serve with chilled applesauce.

The pancakes have a wonderful flavor and can be used either as a first course or as a side dish. Try topping them with a dollop of sour cream rather than applesauce.

Makes: 10 to 12 pancakes, 5 to 6 portions

GRANDMA'S SWEET POTATO SOUFFLE
Souffle de Camote de Abuelita

3 cups cooked camote, mashed   1 T. vanilla
1 cup sugar   1/2 tsp. salt
2 eggs   1/2 tsp. cinnamon
3 1/2 T. butter   1/2 tsp. nutmeg
1/2 cup evaporated milk (can substitute homogenized)

Topping:
1/2 cup light brown sugar   1/3 cup melted butter
1/2 cup dark brown sugar   1 1/2 cups chopped pecans
1/3 cup flour   or walnuts

Beat together all the souffle ingredients and pour into a buttered casserole.

Mix together the topping and pour over the sweet potato mixture. Bake, uncovered, at 350°F for 35 minutes.

The souffle is great dish to accompany holiday meals.

Serves: 4 to 8

YUCA

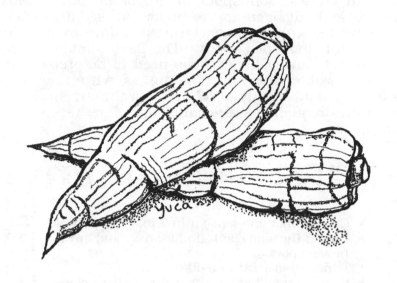

It's yuca, not yucca, in both English and Spanish! A "yucca" is a Southwestern United States desert lily akin to *flor de itabo* while our guide's yuca one of the more than 40 varieties of tropical tubers found in the Americas. The yuca is also referred to in English as cassava or manioc, but most frequently it is simply called "yuca"!

A member of the century-plant family, the yuca is native to arid regions of southern North America, Central America, and to the West Indies. Depending on the species, yuca plants can be squat and nearly stemless or irregularly branched plants as tall as 40 feet.

This fibrous root is long, cylindrical, and tapered at the end. It's size can vary from 4 to 16 inches in length. A bark-like skin covers the bone-white flesh of the yuca. Yuca is always peeled and cooked before being eaten. It's course texture is not unpleasing and the root has a mild, buttery flavor.

Yuca is one of the most versatile tubers. It's the root from which tapioca is made. Yuca yields cassava flour which is used to make a Caribbean flat bread. When boiled, it softens and is used as one would use a potato, in stews, fried, etc.

Although the yuca has a hearty looking appearance, it is frail. When choosing a yuca, avoid those with cracks, soft spots, mold, or an odor. Most yucas are sold cut open so the buyer can see if the flesh is pure white, and it is not unreasonable to ask the vender to cut unopened roots. The flesh should be free of brown spots and veins. Yucas need to be prepared as soon as possible after purchasing as with time they become dry and mealy. Those purchased in North America are frequently wax-coated to reduce this type of spoilage.

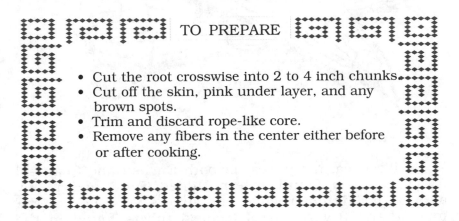

TO PREPARE

- Cut the root crosswise into 2 to 4 inch chunks.
- Cut off the skin, pink under layer, and any brown spots.
- Trim and discard rope-like core.
- Remove any fibers in the center either before or after cooking.

YUCA SALAD
Ensalada de Yuca

2 lbs. yuca, peeled and
  cubed
1/2 cup mayonnaise or to taste
2 hard boiled eggs, chopped
2 medium carrots, peeled, diced,
  and cooked
1 chayote, peeled, cubed, and cooked

1 small cucumber, peeled,
  seeded, and diced
2 medium tomatoes, peeled,
  seeded, and chopped
2 T. capers
Salt and pepper to taste

In a saucepan, cover the yuca with lightly salted water and bring to a boil. Reduce heat and simmer until fork tender, about 20 to 30 minutes. Drain well and let cool.

In a mixing bowl combine the yuca with the mayonnaise and fold in the remaining ingredients. Season with salt and pepper. Chill before serving.

Serves: 6

CHICKEN, YUCA, AND MANGO SALAD
Ensalada de Pollo, Yuca, y Mango

2 whole chicken breasts (about
   2 lbs), with skin and bone
1 lb. fresh yuca, peeled, and cut
   into 3-inch sections
1/3 cup plus 1 T. vegetable oil
3 T. fresh lime juice
1 mango, peeled, pitted, and diced
   into 1/2-inch pieces

6 slices bacon, cooked crisp
   and crumbled
2 T. mayonnaise
1/2 tsp. sugar
1/3 cup chopped red onion
1/2 cup fresh parsley or
   cilantro, chopped
lime slices for garnish

In a pot of salted boiling water, poach the chicken in enough water to cover. Simmer for 15 minutes, or until just cooked through. Let the chicken cool in poaching liquid for 1 hour.

In a large sauce pan combine the yuca with enough water to cover. Bring to a boil, reduce the heat and simmer for 20 to 30 minutes. Transfer the yuca with a slotted spoon to a cutting board and let cool. Cut the yuca lengthwise into 1/2 inch wide wedges, discarding the thin woody core. Cut the wedges crosswise into 1/2 inch thick pieces. In a large bowl, toss the yuca with 1 tablespoon of the oil and 1 tablespoon of the lime juice.

Drain the chicken, discarding the skin and bones; cut the meat into bite size chunks. To the bowl add the chicken, diced mango, and bacon bits.

In a small bowl, whisk together the remaining 1/3 cup oil, the remaining 2 tablespoons lime juice, and the mayonnaise, sugar, and onion. Salt and pepper to taste. Pour the dressing over the salad and toss well, adding the parsley or cilantro. Serve garnished with lime slices.

Serves: 6

YUCA CASSEROLE
Cacerola de Yuca

3 lbs. yuca
1/2 lb. ground beef
1/2 lb. minced ham
1 green bell pepper, chopped
1/2 cup onion, chopped
1/4 cup grated cheese, Turrialba
   or Monterey Jack
1/2 cup celery, chopped

2 garlic cloves, minced
1/4 tsp. ground cumin
1/2 cup bread crumbs
4 T. margarine
4 T. vegetable oil
1 cup of water
1/2 cup tomato sauce
1 cup grated cheese (for top)

131

Peel the yuca, and boil in enough water to cover until done. Remove, drain, and mash as you would potatoes. Mix in 4 tablespoons of butter, 1/4 cup of grated cheese, and salt and pepper to taste.

In a frying pan, heat the vegetable oil. Add the onions, bell pepper, garlic, celery, cumin, ham, and the ground beef. Saute until the meat browns, about 10 minutes. Add the water and tomato sauce and simmer 15 minutes, until the liquid is reduced.

Meanwhile butter a 9 x 13 Pyrex baking dish, then sprinkle it with some of the bread crumbs, about a 1/4 cup.

Divide the mashed yuca into two halves. Put one half on the bottom of the Pyrex dish to form a crust, then add the meat sauce. Next cover the meat sauce with the remaining yuca. Top with grated cheese, bread crumbs, and a few dots of butter. Bake for 30 minutes at 350°F, or until heated through and the top is golden.

Serves: 8 to 10

YUCA CAKE
Queque de Yuca

1 1/2 sticks softened margarine
1 1/4 cups of sugar
4 eggs
3 cups of finely grated raw yuca

2 tsp. baking powder
1/2 cup grated parmesan cheese
1 cup sour cream

With a electric mixer, whip the margarine until fluffy. Add the sugar little by little, continiously beating; then add the eggs, one at a time. Add the 2 cups of cake mix, alternating with the sour cream, beating all together. Add the parmesan cheese and baking powder and beat for 2 minutes more.

Bake in a greased and floured 9 x 13 pyrex dish. Pre-heat the oven to 350°F, and bake the cake for about 30 minutes or until an inserted knife comes out clean.

Serves: 8

ZAPALLO

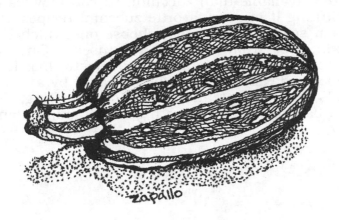

zapallo

The various members of the squash family are generally divided into two categories, winter squash and summer squash. Winter squash have hard thick skins which are not edible and non-edible seeds. Their flesh ranges from deep yellow to orange. They are firmer than summer squash, therefore they require longer cooking. *Calabaza* is a winter squash.

The *zapallo* is a summer squash. Like all summer squash, zapallos have thin edible skins and soft seeds. They have a high water content, so don't require long cooking. Because summer squash are more perishable than winter squash, zapallos do not export well and are rarely seen in North American markets.

There are several varieties of zapallo found Latin America--*zapallo temprano*, *zapallo de guarda*, and *zapallo tipo calabaza*. The variety most prevalent is Costa Rica is akin to the zucchini. Its skin coloring is the same, from dark to light green, with markings that can give it a striped look. The flesh has a similar texture and pale green cast. The flavoring is light and delicate like a zucchini. The principle difference is the round, globe-like shape of the zapallo, although oblong gourd-

133

shaped zapallos are found. A very small variety called *zapallito* (little zapallo) is also available.

In most recipes zucchini and zapallo can be used interchangeably. Here in Central America the zapallo is more readily available than zucchini, so you may want to try substituting it in your favorite zucchini recipes.

When selecting a zapallo, choose one which has a bright skin, free from spots and bruises. Once cut, zapallos need to be refrigerated in a plastic bag for no more than five days. They can be prepared by a number of methods including steaming, grilling, sauteing, deep-frying and baking. Zapallos are high in vitamins A and C as well as niacin.

FRIED ZAPALLO
Zapallo Frito

1/2 cup olive oil
1/2 tsp. salt
1/2 cup corn oil
1/2 tsp. fresh black pepper
3/4 cup unbleached all-purpose flour
3 zucchini or 1 zapallo, cut in
    3 to 4 inch long strips
1/2 tsp. paprika
Lime wedges, for serving

Combine the oils in a skillet, and heat until hot, but not smoking.

Stir together the flour, paprika, salt, and pepper in a mixing bowl.

Dredge the zapallo in the flour mixture, shaking off any excess. Saute it in the hot oil, in batches, until golden and crisp. Drain on paper towels, and serve immediately. Squeeze lots of fresh lime juice over a mountain of these, and let everyone eat them with their fingers as a starter.

Makes: about 4 portions

ZAPALLO AND LEEK SOUP
Sopa de Zapallo y Puerro

2 T. butter or margarine
2 zapallos, finely chopped
3 to 4 leeks, (white part only)
   finely chopped
3 cups milk

1/2 tsp. dry basil
1/4 tsp. thyme
2 tsp. all-purpose flour
Salt and pepper

Melt butter in a 3-quart pan over a medium heat. Add the zapallo, leeks (white part only), basil and thyme. Cook, uncovered, stirring frequently, until the vegetables are tender to bite, about 15 minutes. Stir in the flour and cook about 1 minute, gradually adding the milk. Cook, stirring frequently, until thickened. Season with salt and pepper to taste.

   Cover, and chill before serving. Serve hot, or cool.

   Makes: about 5 cups.

MEXICAN RATATOUILLE
Ratatouille Mexicana

2 T. vegetable oil
1 onion, chopped
2 yellow summer squash (1 1/2
   cups), cut into 1/2 inch cubes
1 zapallo (1 1/2 cups), cut into
   1/2 inch cubes
1 tsp. dried oregano
1/4 cup chopped cilantro

1/2 tsp. ground cumin
Fresh black pepper, to taste
2 green (unripe) tomatoes,
   diced
1 fresh mild chili pepper,
   minced (2 tsp.)
1 jalapeño pepper, minced

   Preheat the oven to 350°F.

   Heat the oil in a large skillet, and sauté the onion over medium heat for about 3 minutes. Add the yellow squash, zucchini, oregano, salt, cumin, and black pepper. Sauté 5 minutes, stirring.

   Stir in the tomatoes and both chilies. Transfer the mixture to an ovenproof 2 1/2 quart casserole, cover, and bake for 30 minutes.

   Stir in the cilantro, and serve immediately or at room temperature.

   Serves: 4 to 6

ZAPALLOS WITH CREAM
Zapallos con Crema

3 medium sized zapallos
1 cup Monterey Jack or Turrialba
  cheese
2 T. butter

4 T. minced onion
1 cup whipping cream
1/4 cup bread crumbs
salt and pepper to taste

Clean and cook the zapallos in boiling, salted water for about 10 minutes. Drain and rinse in cold water. Saute the onions in a little butter.

Preheat the oven to 350°F. Butter an 8-inch square pyrex baking dish. Cut the zapallos into diagonal slices. Layer half the slices, top with half the minced onion, half the cheese, half the cream, and half the bread crumbs. Sprinkle with salt to taste. Repeat with another layer. Dot the top with butter and bake uncovered for 30 minutes, until the cheese melts.

Serves: 6

ZAPALLO OMELETTE
Torta de Zapallo

1 medium zapallo, grated
1/2 tsp. ground oregano
1 tsp. fresh basil, chopped
2 T. flour
1 small onion, grated

4 eggs, lightly beaten
1 cup grated cheddar cheese
2 tsp. cooking oil
salt and pepper to taste

Heat the cooking oil in a heavy frying pan. In a mixing bowl, blend all the ingredients evenly together. Pour the mixture into the frying pan and cover. Cook until the omelette is set.

To serve, flip the omelette over on to a plate. Serve with a salad and fresh bread for a light meal or as a side dish.

Serves: 6

OTHER REGIONAL VEGETABLES

 Below are descriptions of some other vegetables often used in Central America cooking. Vegetables well-known to English speakers are listed in our section, **Spanish Names For Common North American Foods.**

Calabaza: A term covering all types of squash. *Calabacitas*, or small squash, are equivalent to zucchini. *Calabaza* is also the Spanish word for pumpkin.

Chiles picantes: There are more than 200 varieties of hot peppers, over 100 of which are indigenous to Mexico. There are not very many varieties found in Costa Rica, and their availability varies according to the season. With some looking, *Habaneros* (scotch bonnet peppers) and *jalapeños* can be found...perhaps not fresh but canned or dried. *Habanereos* are one of the hottest chilies. *Jalapeños*, known as *chipotles* in their dried form, are flavorful and easily seeded. As a general rule: the larger the chile, the milder the flavor. Other well-known hot peppers are the *ancho*, the *serrano*, and the *poblano*.

Epazote: Wormseed in English and called *culantro coyote* in Costa Rica. Fresh leaves are used as a flavoring in soups, tacos, and beans. The plant has medicinal qualities.

Flor de Itabo: Bell-shaped white flowers from the Itabo plant. Since they are bitter in taste the flowers must be boiled several times before being utilized in a dish. They can be used to flavor omelettes or soups or can be fried in butter.

Haba: A big lima bean which is served as a vegetable or used in soups and sauces.

Name: A tuber with a brown skin which looks much like a russet potato. The raw interior is white or cream colored and wet and sticky, but when cooked the texture is like a potato and the taste has a hint of chestnut.

Ñampi: A tropical tuber with a nut-like flavor. Known as taro root in English, it is like a potato, but a little sweeter.

Nopales: Cactus leaves--flat, thin, and broad in shape. They are rarely found in Costa Rica. They are abundant in Mexico where they are sold cleaned of their spines in most markets. Nopales have a refreshing sweet/sour flavor and are rich in vitamins and mineral salts.

Pacaya: The edible part of a palm which looks like a corn husk, but is actually a palm flower. To prepare it, you must remove the head from the green covering and boil it to neutralize the bitterness. Eat it plain with butter, pickle it, or use it in omelets.

Papa: The Spanish name for potato. Thick skin baking potatoes, like the Russet, are not available in Costa Rica. Most typically only thin skinned white and sometimes red varieties are found.

Quelite: This plant looks like spinach and is cooked and prepared like spinach!

Tiquisque: A tropical tuber from the cassava/yuca family. It has a brown peel and white pulp, speckled with purple. Use tiquisques as you would other tubers.

Tomate: You do not find a wide variety of tomatoes in Costa Rica. The common garden-variety is available. Cherry tomatoes and plum tomatos can sometimes be found.

BEANS/FRIJOLES

Bean, *frijol* in Spanish, is the common name for a number of leguminous plants and their seeds, family *Leguminosae*, and for several other unrelated species. There are black beans (turtle beans), kidney beans (red beans), white beans (Navy, Great Northern, and Cannellini beans), pinto beans, broad beans (fava beans), cranberry beans, and more. Lima beans, chick-peas (garbanzos), black-eyed peas, and soybeans are all related.

Beans are a staple in the diet of peoples throughout the world. They are affordable, rich in protein, and high in soluble fiber which helps lower blood cholesterol levels. The bean is the corner stone of Hispanic cooking, however, today a new generation of American chefs has rediscovered the bean, and it has risen to stardom in the kitchens of elegant North American restaurants.

The best known beans in Central America are the red bean and the black bean. Both are indigenous to the area and were widely disseminated in North and South America prior to European exploration.

Bean plants are annuals with a bush-type or twining-type growth habit. The fruit is a pod containing several white, red, or dark seeds. Depending on the bean, the pod may be round, oval, or flat in shape, and green, yellow, or red in color.

Black beans, *frijoles negros*, are sometimes called turtle beans. They are small, mild flavored, kidney-shaped beans with a tiny white eye and a white interior. They have an earthy flavor which reminds some of mushrooms. They are used extensively in Mexican, Central American, and Caribbean cooking.

The kidney bean, *frijol rojo*, has several varieties which range in color from pink to dark-red. The dark-red variety is the true kidney. The pinto bean, a smaller pale pink speckled bean, is utilized in Mexican cooking as it is in the regional fare of Southwestern United States.

Dried beans can be purchased in bulk just about everywhere--in the Central Market, at *ferias*, at mini-supers, and at the supermarket. Frequently, bags will contain pebbles and other foreign matter, so you will want to rinse the beans thoroughly before using.

Traditionally beans have been utilized in soups, stews, and a number of side dishes, like chili. Increasingly, modern chefs are turning to beans as an ingredient in exotic salads and salsas.

Dried beans are rich in protein, calcium, phosphorus, and iron. Their high protein content, along with the fact that they're easily grown and stored, has made beans one Central America's favorite staples!

COOKING BEANS

1. Sort the beans carefully, removing stones and debris.
2. Wash and drain the beans in a colander.
3. Place the beans in a large pot with an ample amount of water and let them soak over night.
4. Drain the water and wash the beans once again.
5. Return the beans to the pot and add some minced garlic, onion and bell pepper to season.
6. Add water to cover, bring to a boil, then reduce heat and simmer covered until tender, about 2 1/2 hours.
7. Add extra hot water as needed and salt and pepper to taste.

BLACK BEAN SALSA
Salsa de Frijoles Negros

2 cups Firm-Cooked Black Beans
(See recipe below)
2 to 3 T. extra-virgin olive oil
3 to 4 T. fresh lime juice, to taste
1/2 cup cooked corn kernels
1 ripe avocado, finely diced
1 poblano chili or 1/2 green bell
    pepper, cored, seeded, finely diced
Salt and black pepper to taste

1/2 red bell pepper, cored,
    seeded, and finely diced
1/2 cup diced red onion
1 or 2 jalapeño chilies,
    seeded and minced
1/2 tsp. ground cumin
1/2 cup finely chopped fresh
    cilantro or mint leaves

Combine all of the ingredients in a mixing bowl and toss well. Correct the seasonings, adding salt or lime juice to taste. The salsa should be highly seasoned. Serve with plantain chips or tortilla chips.

Serves: 4 to 6

FIRM-COOKED BLACK BEANS
Frijoles Negros Cocidos

1 lb. dried black beans, picked
    through and washed
1 sm. onion, cut in half
2 ribs celery, cut into 2-inch pieces
2 carrots, cut into 2-inch pieces
1/2 green pepper, cored & seeded
3 cloves garlic, peeled

1 bouquet garni (1 bay leaf, 3
    sprigs fresh thyme or 1/2
    tsp. dried, and 3 sprigs
    parsley tied in cheesecloth)
1/2 tsp. ground cumin
1/2 tsp. dried oregano
salt and pepper to taste

In a large heavy pot, soak the beans in cold water to cover by at least 3 inches for no less than 4 hours, or overnight. (If omitting this step, add approximately 1 hour to the cooking time.)

Add the vegetables, garlic, bouquet garni, cumin, and oregano to the pot of beans and soaking water. Bring to a boil over a high heat. Skim off any foam which rises to the surface.

Reduce the heat and gently simmer the beans, uncovered, stirring occasionally, until tender, 1 to 1 3/4 hours. Add water as necessary to keep the beans submerged.

Season the beans with salt and pepper during the last 10 minutes of cooking. Drain the beans in a colander and rinse with cold water. Remove and discard the vegetables and bouquet garni.

The beans are now ready for adding to salads or salsas or to be used in *gallo pinto*. They can be stored, covered, in the refrigerator for up to 3 days. The beans can also be reheated in a skillet or saucepan.

Makes: 4 to 5 cups

141

BLACK BEAN SOUP
Sopa de Frijoles Negros

Beans:

1 lb. dried black beans
1/2 green pepper, cored & seeded
2 cloves garlic
1 bay leaf
1 small onion, cut in half
1 whole clove

Soup:

5 oz. bacon, cut into 1/4 inch slivers
3 T. exta-virgin olive oil
1 large onion, finely chopped
1 green bell pepper, cored, seeded,
  and finely chopped
1 carrot, finely chopped
4 cloves garlic, minced
2 ribs celery, finely chopped
1/2 cup dry white wine
1 T. wine vinegar
1 tsp. ground cumin
1 tsp. dried oregano
2 bay leaves
Salt and pepper to taste
1/4 cup sour cream,
  for garnish
1/4 cup finely chopped
  scallions for garnish

Prepare the beans: The day before spread the beans on a baking sheet and pick through them, removing any foreign substances. Rinse the beans thoroughly in a strainer under cold running water. Place the beans in a large heavy pot and add 8 cups of water. Let soak overnight in the refrigerator.

Add the bell pepper and garlic to the pot. Pin the bay leaf to the onion with the clove, and add it to the pot. Bring the water to a boil. Reduce the heat, loosely cover the pan, and simmer the beans , stirring occasionally, until tender, about 1 hour. (The beans can also be cooked in a 6-quart pressure cooker for about 30 to 40 minutes.)

Prepare the soup: Brown the bacon in a large heavy frying pan, 3 to 4 minutes. Using a slotted spoon, transfer the bacon to paper towels to drain. Pour off the fat from the pan.

Add the olive oil to the pan, followed by the onion, bell pepper, carrot, celery, and garlic. Cook over medium heat until the vegetables are soft but not brown, 4 to 5 minutes.

Stir the sauteed vegetables and bacon into the beans, along with the wine, vinegar, cumin, oregano, bay leaves, and salt and pepper. Cover and gently simmer the soup until the beans are very soft, 10 to 15 minutes.

Remove and discard the bay leaves. Using a slotted spoon, transfer 2 cups of the beans to a bowl and mash with the back of a wooden spoon or a pestle. Stir this mixture back into the soup to give it a creamy consistency. Correct the seasonings, adding salt, pepper, or vinegar to taste.

Ladle the soup into bowls and garnish each with a dollop of the sour cream and a sprinkling of the scallion greens. The soup can also be topped with thin hard boiled egg slices.

Serves: 8

BEAN DIP
Dip de Frijoles

1 lb. red or black beans, cooked   1 tsp. chili powder
    and drained   1/8 tsp. ground cumin
2 T. green bell pepper, finely chopped   1 tsp. jalapeño pepper
2 tsp. minced onion, sauteed lightly   2 tsp. minced fresh parsley
1 T. vinegar

Put the beans, peppers, vinegar , chili powder, and ground cumin in the blender. Blend until smooth. Transfer the mixture to a bowl. Add the onion and parsley, and sprinkle the top with grated Parmesan cheese. Serve with tortilla chips.
Makes: Approximately 2 cups

REFRIED BEANS
Frijoles Refritos

1 lb. red or black beans   1 green pepper , minced
9 to 10 cups of water   1 tsp. salt
1 T. cooking oil   2 cloves garlic
    (Added to reduce foam)   2 T. cooking oil
1 medium onion, quartered   2 leaves of *cilantro coyote*
1 small onion, minced   (epazote/wormseed)

Sort and rinse the beans, then soak overnight in water. The next day, add the quartered onion, garlic, and oil. Put in a heavy sauce pan, and bring to a boil over a high heat. Reduce the heat and simmer for about 1 1/2 hours.
Stir the salt into the beans, and cook for another 45 minutes or until tender, adding more water as needed.
Heat the two tablespoons of oil in a saute pan. Sauté the minced onion and green pepper for about 4 minutes.
In a blender, put 3 cups of the cooked beans and 1 cup of the broth, and puree. Repeat until all the beans are pureed.
Add the beans to the mixture in the saute pan. Mix together, adding more broth if needed to adjust the thickness. Simmer, stirring frequently, for about 15 to 20 minutes.
Serves: 6

CHICK-PEA/GARBANZO

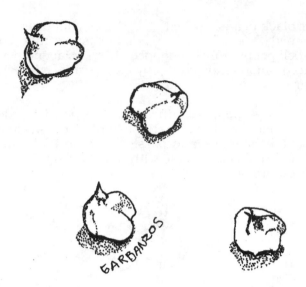

Where in the world did this bean acquire the name, chick-pea? No doubt it was an evolutionary process from the Roman word *cicer* to the French *pois chiche*, and finally to the English who began to call it *chich pea*. Of course, the bean has absolutely no connection to chickens!! Although some may refer to the bean as the chick-pea, most commonly in North America it is called by its Spanish name, *garbanzo*, or in some regions "Spanish bean".

The garbanzo, like other beans and peas, is a member of the *Leguminosae* family. The bean is indigenous to the Mediterranean area, and has been cultivated there since ancient times. It is utilized extensively in Middle Eastern cuisine, but through the centuries the garbanzo bean has found its way into Spanish and Italian dishes. There is little doubt the Spanish were responsible for the bean's introduction into the New World.

Garbanzo beans are extensively grown in Central and South America and have found their way into regional soups, stews, and other dishes. With the rise of Southwestern cuisine in the United States, garbanzos have been put to new and unique uses, principally in salads.

The garbanzo is slightly larger than the average pea, round, irregular-shaped, and buff-colored. It has a firm texture and a mild, nut-like flavor. Garbanzos are found both fresh and canned in Costa Rica. To prepare fresh garbanzos, they must be cooked as you would other beans.

GARBANZO, GARLIC, AND PARSLEY DIP
Dip de Garbanzo, Ajo, y Perejil

2 cups cooked garbanzo beans, or 19 oz.
   can, drained
1/2 cup packed fresh parsley, washed
   and spun dry
2 garlic cloves, chopped and mashed to a
   paste
1/4 cup water
3 T. fresh lime juice
1/2 tsp. salt
1/4 cup extra-virgin olive oil

In a food processor blend all the ingredients except the oil until smooth. With the motor running add the oil in a slow steam. Season the dip with salt.

Serve the dip on toasted pita wedges or toasted French bread slices.

Makes: about 2 cups

GARBANZO AND OLIVE VINAIGRETTE
Vinaigrette de Garbanzos y Aceitunas

1 T. olive oil
1 tsp. white wine vinegar
1 tsp. Dijon mustard
1 16 to 19 oz. can garbanzos,
   rinsed and drained

3 oz. jar pimento-stuffed
   olives (about 1/2 cup)
   drained and sliced
1 T. minced fresh parsley
freshly ground black pepper

In a bowl whisk together oil, vinegar, and mustard. Add the garbanzos, olives, parsley, pepper, and salt to taste. Toss to combine.

Serves: 2

WARM GARBANZO AND GREEN MANGO SALAD
Ensalada Caliente de Garbanzo y Mango Verde

1 small green mango
1 1/2 T. mild vegetable oil
1/2 tsp. mustard seeds
2 dried red chilies, stemmed and
   broken into pieces
2 cups garbanzos, freshly cooked
   or canned and drained

2 T. grated fresh coconut
   (or defrosted frozen)
1/2 tsp. salt or to taste
1 small avocado
lettuce leaves, washed and
   crisped

Wash the mango and cut off the blossom end. Grate on a hard grater. Do not peel. Discard the pit.

Heat the oil in a sauce pan over medium heat. Add the mustard seed and chilies. When the seeds sputter, add the mango, garbanzos, and coconut. Add the salt. Sir and cook until warm.

Line a shallow bowl with lettuce leaves and mound the salad in the center. Peel and pit the avocado, then cut it into 1/2 inch slices. Scatter over the salad.

Serves: 4

GARBANZOS AND PORK
Garbanzos y Cerdo

2 (16 oz.) cans garbanzos
   with their juice
1 lb. pork shoulder, cubed
1 red bell pepper, chopped
2 cloves garlic, finely chopped
1 medium onion, chopped
1 celery rib, chopped

1 sprig parsley
2 12 oz. cans beef broth
3 medium carrots, cubed
3 medium potatoes, cubed
4 T. cooking oil
Salt and achiote to taste

Heat the cooking oil in a heavy pot. Brown the pork shoulder in the oil. Add the garlic, peppers, and onion, and saute until translucent. Add the garbanzo liquid and the two cans of beef broth. Cover and simmer for one hour or until the meat is fork tender. Add the cubed carrots and potatoes, cooking for about 20 additional minutes. Finally, add the garbanzos and heat.

Serves: 4

RICE/ARROZ

     Since ancient times, rice, *arroz* in Spanish, has been the most commonly used food grain for the majority of people in the world. A member of the grass family, rice, *oryza sativa*, is grown successfully under almost any climatic conditions as long as the plants have a steady supply of water either by excessive rainfall or irrigation.

     Rice, both the plant and the word, is oriental in origin. Archaeological explorations in China have uncovered sealed pots of rice that are almost 8,000 years old. The Arabs introduced rice to the Mediterranean area where it has become a prominent food crop. Most likely, the Spanish and Portuguese are responsible for the introduction of rice to the New World.

     Botanically more than 7,000 different varieties of rice have been identified. Rice is commercially classified by its size--long, medium, and short grain. In each type, the amount of moisture varies. Long-grain rices are often preferred over short or medium grains because they have the least moisture and less tendency to stick together when cooked. They are best for salads and dishes where each grain should be separate and fluffy. One of the more exotic varieties is the perfumy East Indian Basmati rice.

Short and medium grain rices have more moisture and are more glutinous and sticky when cooked. Short-grain rices, also called pearl rices, have the highest starch content. Short-grains are best used in molds, casseroles, croquettes, and puddings. A special Italian short grain, Arborio, is used to make creamy risottos.

Rice can be further divided into two other broad categories--brown and white. Brown rice is the entire grain with only the inedible husk removed. It has greater nutritional value than white rice, but it needs to be cooked longer because it retains it high-fiber bran coating. The bran also gives brown rice a nut-like favor and a more chewy texture than white rice. Brown rice, *arroz intregal,* is available in Costa Rica.

White rice has been "milled" to remove the husk and bran. A problem locally is determining if the white rice you are purchasing is long grain or short grain. Most often in Central America the type of grain is not indicated on the bag label.

Wild rice, prized for its nutty flavor and firm, chewy texture, is really not a rice, but the seed of a grass. Converted rices or parboiled rices are rices where the unhulled grain has been soaked, pressure-steamed and dried before milling. This treatment infuses some of the nutrients of the bran back into the kernel's heart and gives converted rice a pale beige cast. In our opinion, instant rices (rices which have been fully or partially cooked before being dehydrated) are to be avoided because they have lackluster flavor and texture!

Local rices always need to be rinsed well before using, not only to take some of the starch out, but to remove impurities. Those desiring good quality rices can find Arborio, Basmati, and other fine imported rices at some of the more upscale supermarkets.

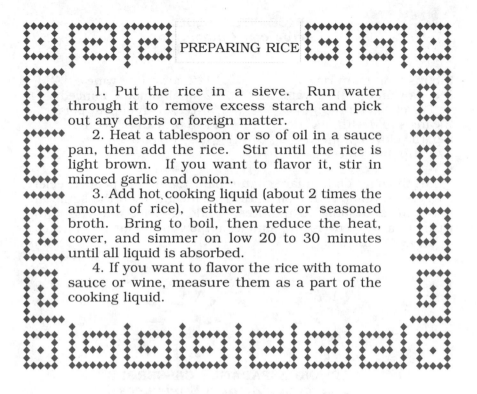

PREPARING RICE

1. Put the rice in a sieve. Run water through it to remove excess starch and pick out any debris or foreign matter.

2. Heat a tablespoon or so of oil in a sauce pan, then add the rice. Stir until the rice is light brown. If you want to flavor it, stir in minced garlic and onion.

3. Add hot cooking liquid (about 2 times the amount of rice), either water or seasoned broth. Bring to boil, then reduce the heat, cover, and simmer on low 20 to 30 minutes until all liquid is absorbed.

4. If you want to flavor the rice with tomato sauce or wine, measure them as a part of the cooking liquid.

SEAFOOD RICE EL SOL
Arroz con Mariscos El Sol

3 cups cooked rice
1/4 cup minced onion
4 T. minced bell pepper
1 clove garlic, minced
4 T. minced celery
3 T. tomato sauce
1 T. chicken consommé powder

18 small mussels
18 small clams
24 small to medium shrimp
1/4 cup cubed sea bass
1/4 cup olive oil
1/2 cup white wine

Heat the olive oil in a frying pan. Saute the onions, peppers, garlic, and celery for about 5 minutes. Add all the fish, except the shrimp. Then add the tomato sauce, consommé powder and rice. Mix well. Finally, add the wine and shrimp. Heat thoroughly... and serve.

Serves: 4 to 6

RICE WITH SQUID
Arroz con Calamares

3 cups long grain rice
5 cups water (or 1/2 water and
   1/2 chicken broth)
2 cans squid with ink
5 garlic cloves, minced
1/2 cup minced celery

1/2 cup white wine
2 small onions, minced
1 6 oz. can of petit pois
1 6 oz. can pimentos
1/4 cup olive oil

Put the olive oil in a large saute pan. Saute the pepper, celery, garlic, and onion in the oil until translucent. Add the squid and saute an additional 5 minutes. Add the rice and the liquid. Bring to a boil, cover, and simmer on low for about 20 minutes.

Serves: 8 to 10

RICE AND ASPARAGUS CASSEROLE
Cacerola de Arroz y Espárragos

2 cups long grain rice
2 T. cooking oil
1 medium onion, finely chopped
3 garlic cloves, minced
4 T. grated Parmesan cheese
8 oz. sliced Turrialba or Monterey Jack cheese

1 cup whipping cream or
   half and half
16 oz. can asparagus spears
2 cups chicken or beef broth
1/2 cup grated Parmesan

Saute the garlic and onion in the cooking oil. Remove from pan when slightly browned. Add the rice to the remaining oil, and saute for 5 minutes, until gold in color. Add the broth and asparagus juice to make four cups of liquid. Bring to a boil, reduce heat and cover, simmering until the rice is cooked, about 20 minutes.

In a greased 9 x 11 pyrex baking dish, put a layer of rice, a layer or cheese slices, and a layer of asparagus spears. Top with Parmesan cheese and cream. Repeat the layering until all ingredients are used, ending with Parmesan cheese on the top.

Bake in a 350°F oven for 30 minutes.

Serves: 8 to 10

SWEET CORN/ELOTE

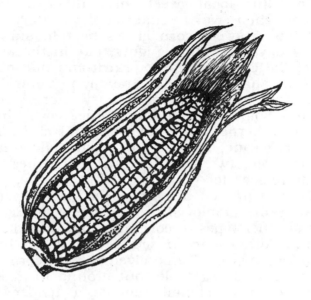

Strictly speaking corn, *zea mays*, is not a vegetable, but a grain. An annual plant of the grass family, *Gramneae*, corn is native to the Americas. The exact place of corn's origin is yet to be determined, although it is thought to be in Mexico or Peru. Corn was unknown outside the New World until 1492, but has been cultivated and utilized as a food product from the Andes to New England for many centuries. In fact, archaeological evidence and measures of radioactive decay indicate corn was cultivated in Mexico at least 7,000 years ago!

Seed grains of Indian corn were brought to Europe by 16th century explorers. Corn has subsequently been planted and now thrives throughout most of the world. Since the 1930's, the development of hybrid varieties has resulted in increased yields and improved the quality.

Our guide deals with sweet corn, *elote* in Spanish, because it is the most edible corn variety, the type found "on-the-cob" in markets. The two most frequently found sweet corns are "Country Gentleman", or white corn, and "Golden Bantam", yellow corn. White corn kernels

151

are smaller and sweeter than yellow corn kernels. Both white and yellow corn are found in Costa Rica, however we do not find local sweet corns to be as milky and tender as their North American counterparts. An explanation is sweet corn grows best in sunny climes with long days and short nights, like in the Midwestern region of the United States. Environmental differences, such as the shorter length of the day in Central America, may explain the poorer quality here. To insure tenderness, some prefer to buy canned corn. In addition to its use in kernel form, *elote*, ground and mixed with lard or margarine, is used to prepare *chorreadas* and *tamal de elote*, two popular "*tipico*" dishes. (We are including recipes for both!)

Some varieties of corn, because of their texture and starch, are employed as feed for livestock while the kernels of other types of corn are used to make popcorn, flour, and other corn-based products. In Central America, *maíz* is the name given to field corn. *Maíz* is never eaten as a vegetable, but ground to make *masa*, the local cornmeal. Finally, *chilote*, a tender baby corn which can be eaten whole, is corn variety also available in Costa Rica. It's found bottled and sometimes pickled in supermarkets. *Chilotes* are great to put in soups and stews.

When selecting corn, look for ears with bright green, snugly fitting husks and golden brown silk. The kernels should be plump and milky, and come all the way to the ear's tip. The rows of kernels should be tightly spaced. As soon as it is picked, corn's sugar begins to turn to starch. The corn begins to toughen and lose its sweetness, thus fresh corn should be cooked and served as soon as possible after picking.

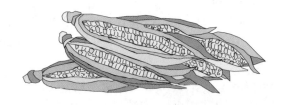

SWEET AND SOUR CORN RELISH
Condimento Agri-dulce de Elote

5 ears fresh corn
1 1/2 cups chopped red onions
1 cup chopped red bell pepper
3 cups white wine vinegar
1/2 cup sugar

1 tsp. mustard seeds
1 tsp. celery seeds
1 T. coarse (kosher) salt
1 T. coarse black pepper

Cut the kernels off the ears of corn.

Combine the corn kernels with all the remaining ingredients in a large sauce saucepan. Bring to a boil, then reduce the heat and simmer until the mixture thickens slightly, about 40 minutes. Set aside to cool, then transfer the relish to storage jars and refrigerate until ready to serve--but no longer than 1 week.

This recipe makes a bunch! Serve the relish alongside your favorite burgers or with a bowl of chili. It can also be used as a garnish for grilled meats and poultry.

Makes: 6 cups

CORN SOUP
Sopa de Elote

3 ears of corn or 1 1/2 cups
   whole kernel canned corn
1 garlic clove
1/2 tsp. salt
1 T. butter
1 small onion, chopped
cilantro leaves

3 small tomatoes, peeled,
   seeded, and chopped
1 quart chicken or beef broth
1/2 tsp. dry leaf oregano
1/4 cup whipping cream
   or milk

Cut the corn kernels from the cob. Measure the corn--you will need about 1 1/2 cups. Purée 3/4 cup corn in the blender and set aside. Mash the garlic with the salt to make a paste. Melt the butter in a large saucepan, then add the onions and the garlic paste. Cook until the onion is tender, but not brown.

Add the tomatoes. Cook the tomatoes slowly for 10 minutes, mashing them with a fork. Then add the broth, oregano, pureed corn, and the whole kernel corn and bring to a boil. Reduce the heat, cover, and simmer for about 30 minutes.

Stir in the cream and cook until hot. To serve, garnish with the cilantro.

Servings: 6

CORN PANCAKES
Chorreadas

6 ears of fresh, tender corn
3 eggs
1 cup of grated cheese--Turrialba
   or Monterey Jack
2 T. sour cream

1/2 cup flour
1/2 stick margarine or
   or butter, melted
2 T. sugar
Oil for frying

Put all the ingredients except the cooking oil into a blender and mix for about 5 minutes. Then in a heavy frying pan, pour tablespoon or so of the mixture as you would when making pancakes.

Chorreadas can be a breakfast item, a first course for a meal, or can be eaten alone. They are usually served topped with dollops of sour cream.

Makes: 4 to 6

CORN STEW
Pozol

1 lb. maiz cascado (hominy)
1 lb. lean pork shoulder
2 chicken breasts
2 green bell peppers
1 small jalapeño pepper
2 tomatoes, chopped
1 medium onion, minced

2 stalks celery, minced
1 bunch *cilantro coyote*,
   (epazote/wormseed),
   chopped
2 cubes chicken bouillon
4 cloves garlic
1/2 tsp. oregano
1 tsp. salt

The day before, in a large pot, cook the corn with the pork, garlic, and chicken bouillon, adding water to cover, about 6 to 8 cups. Cook for 25 minutes. Add the chicken breasts, tomatoes, oregano, and salt, and cook for about 40 minutes more. Remove the meats from the liquid and cube.

Meanwhile, saute the onion, jalapeño, celery, and garlic. Then add the cubed meats and corn with its broth.

Serve in bowls garnished with chopped oregano, radish slices, chopped onion, chopped lettuce, lime slices, etc.

Serves: 8 to 10

TICO CORN BREAD
Tamal de Elote

1 stick of butter or margarine
10 ears of corn, with kernels
    grated from the ear
1/2 lb. vegetable shortening
1 1/2 cups sugar

1 cup flour
1 T. baking powder
6 eggs
2 cups grated white cheese
pinch of salt

Grate the corn. Beat the eggs and mix with the corn.

On the stove top melt the butter and shortening, then cool and mix with the eggs.

Sift together the flour, baking powder, and sugar. Combine the two mixes. Add the cheese until thoroughly mixed without beating the mixture too much. Best to beat it by hand.

Pour the mixture into a greased and floured 9 x 13 pyrex baking dish. Bake at 350°F for 30 minutes, or until golden and an inserted knife comes out clean.

Serve with coffee as a dessert or as a snack.

Serves: 8 to 10

MEAT CUTS AND PRODUCTS

In comparison to North America, most meats are more reasonably priced in Costa Rica, however the cuts may not always be precisely comparable. So that our readers are in a better position to choose the meat cut they desire, we include illustrations which will help when ordering beef and pork.

Guanacaste is the "Texas" of Costa Rica! The presence of this beef producing region makes beef readily available, but many will find the Guanacastan beef on the tough side. Unlike in North America, beef is not aged in Central America. A marinade on beef to be grilled or broiled will help, while beef to be boiled for stews and other stove top dishes generally must be cooked longer in order to become tender. The locals sometimes utilize MSG as a meat tenderizer!

Veal and lamb are difficult to find in Costa Rica as little is produced domestically. If you must have them, we suggest you visit a quality meat market like Don Fernando's in Escazú.

BEEF

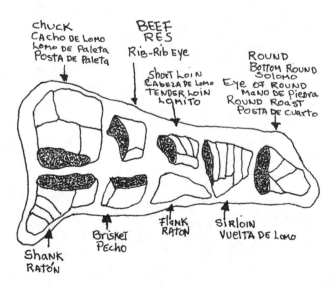

BEEF PRODUCTS (*Carne de res*)

brisket	pecho
chuck	posta
ground meat, hamburger	carne molida
meatballs	albóndigas
oxtail	cola de buey
roast	rosbif
shank	ratón
steak	lomo, lomito
stew meat	posta papa sudar
sweetbreads	mollejas
testicles	criadillas
tongue	lengua
tripe (stomach & intestines)	mondongo

PORK

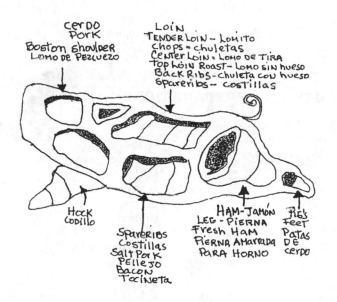

cerDO
PorK

Boston shoulder
LOMO DE PEZCUEZO

LOIN
TENDER LOIN - LOMITO
chops = chuletas
Center LOIN = LOMO DE TIRA
Top LOIN Roast - Lomo sin hueso
Back Ribs - chuleta con hueso
spareribs - costillas

HocK
codillo

Spareribs
Costillas
Salt PorK
PEllejo
Bacon
Tocineta

HAM - Jamón
LEG - PiERNA
Fresh HaM
PiERNA AMarrada
PaRa HORNO

Pig's
FeeT
Patas
DE
cerDO

PORK PRODUCTS (*Cerdo*)

bacon	tocino
chop	chuleta
ham	jamón
patas de puerco	pig's feet
ribs	costillas
salt pork	pellejo
sausage	salchicha, chorizo

OTHER MEATS

goat	cabrito
lamb	cordero
rabbit	conejo
suckling pig	lechón
veal	ternera
venison	venado

OTHER CUTS AND PREPARATIONS

brains	sesos
cold cuts	flambres, carnes frías
flank	falda
kidneys	riñones
leg	pierna, pata
liver	higado
liverwurst	paté
skins/cracklings	chicharrones

POULTRY CUTS AND PRODUCTS

 Chicken is readily available in Costa Rica and quite reasonable. Prior to the last several years, all turkeys were imported. Turkeys are now being raised locally and steadily dropping in price. On occasion duck can be found, but it is imported.

TYPES OF POULTRY

chicken	pollo
duck	pato
turkey	pavo
skinless	sin pellejo
boneless	deshuesado

POULTRY CUTS

entero	whole
medio	split or half
cuarto	quarter
pierna, pata	leg
pechuga	breast
muslo	thigh
alas	wings

FISH AND SEAFOOD

Fresh fish and seafood are not as abundant in Costa Rica as one would expect. We suggest you buy your fish at a *pescadería* (fish market) the morning of the day you plan to cook it. Fish in supermarkets and especially mini-supers cannot always be counted on to be "today's catch".

If you are a lover of shellfish, you will find lobster, prawns, and jumbo shrimp, as elsewhere, quite expensive. Squid and octopus are available locally and are more reasonably priced. Places like Yoahan stock frozen, imported fish and seafood, such as Chilean salmon and King and Dungeness crab.

Sea bass, *corvina*, is the most frequently found white fish in Costa Rica. It's great just pan fried, or it can be prepared with a variety of sauces and stuffings. *Corvina* is the white fish most typically used in the preparation of *ceviche*. Related to tuna and bluefish is Spanish mackerel, *macarela,* which abounds on Costa Rica's Atlantic coast. It's an oily fish, so most prefer to bake it, although it can be filleted and fried. *Pargo*, snapper in English, is also found in Costa Rican waters. It's fantastic filleted and equally as good whole. At some locales red tuna is available for a very reasonable price. You can broil the tuna steaks, or if you like the fresh tuna can be eaten raw in appetizers and salads.

In addition to fresh fish, canned fish, both domestic and imported, is widely available. Mussels, clams, and other delicacies are stocked at quality supermarkets. Learn to read the labels as many items come with seasonings and other "goodies" added For example, you will not want to bring home *atún escabeche* (tuna with pickled vegetables) for your tuna casserole! High quality water packed tuna from coastal waters would be a better purchase.

Remember this golden rule when purchasing fresh fish or seafood: "If it smells, don't buy it!".

FISH--PESCADOS

cod	bacalao (usually comes dried and salted)
dolphin, mahi-mahi	dorado
mackerel	macarela
red snapper	pargo rojo
sea bass	corvina
salmon	salmón
sardines	sardinas
shark	tiburón
trout	trucha
tuna	atún
turtle	tortuga

SEAFOOD--MARISCOS

clams	almejas
crayfish	langostinos
lobster	langosta
mussels	mejillones
octopus	pulpo
oysters	ostiones
prawns	camarones jumbos
shrimp	camarones
squid	calamares

MAKING TORTILLAS

As most undoubtedly know, tortillas are flat corn or flour based "pancakes" which are served hot as "bread" or utilized to prepare a variety of dishes. They are the "backbone" of Central American cooking. Among other things, tortillas can be stuffed, rolled, layered, fried, or served with toppings! Tortillas can vary in size, thickness, and texture from one Central American country to another. Although flour tortillas can be found, in Costa Rica tortillas most typically are make from corn meal.

The name "tortilla" comes from the diminutive form of the Spanish *torta*, "round cake". The tortilla was first introduced to English speakers in the chronicles of the late 17th century travelers to the New World. However, tortillas did not really become a part of North American cuisine until the current century when they have been utilized extensively in Tex-Mex fare and Southwestern cooking.

For those readers wanting to immerse themselves in regional cooking, we provide you instructions for making tortillas. They are really quite simple to make, and you can bet your fresh homemade tortillas will be tastier than those dry and flaky packaged ones found in the supermarket!

CORN TORTILLAS
Tortillas de maiz

2 cups Masa Rica (purchased at any supermarket)
1 to 1 1/2 cups warm water
1 tortilla press (purchased at supermarkets or household goods stores)

Steps:

1. Mix the masa with the water is a large bowl, adding more water if needed, a tablespoon at a time. Knead to form a nice stiff dough.

2. Cut two 8-inch squares of plastic wrap and put one onto the bottom of a tortilla press.

3. Divide the dough into 12 pieces for 6-inch tortillas and into about 24 pieces for 4-inch tortillas.

4. Make 2-inch balls from the dough, flattening slightly. Place each on top of the plastic wrap, a little off the center of the press. Put the second piece of plastic wrap on top. Then, PRESS!

5. Heat an ungreased tortilla pan or heavy skillet over a medium heat until water dances on it when sprinkled. Cook each tortilla 1 minute on each side, or until it slightly puffs. Push down with a spatula and turn to cook the remaining side.

6. After removing the tortillas from the griddle, stack them and cover with aluminum foil. They will keep under refrigeration up to 4 days.

CENTRAL AMERICAN FAVORITES

Many of these "Central American Favorites" rely heavily on staples which are familiar to North American cooks, but regional dishes also utilize tropical tubers, vegetables, and spices which may not be so familiar. A number of our selections are not exactly healthy low calorie or low cholesterol items, and some rely on frying. What they may lack in nutrition is offset by their unique "tastes". We include these Central American favorites because they are the Latin equivalents of meat loaf and apple pie!

Central American cooking is very distinctive from Mexican and American Southwestern cuisine. We provide you with a "sampler" to enrich your entertaining and perhaps even your everyday meals. Some are simple and quick dishes, others more complex, but rewarding. Remember, one of the best ways to experience a culture is through your stomach...so enjoy with *Sabor!*

COSTA RICAN TAMALES...

Tamales can be found year around in Costa Rica, but they are the traditional food at Christmas. Each family has its own special recipe for the stuffing. The *tamal* is made with *masa*, a bleached ground corn flour, seasoned with herbs. Either chicken or pork is the stuffing base. Other stuffing ingredients can include rice made yellow with achiote, pieces of hard boiled egg, peas, diced carrots, diced potatoes, olives, raisins, and sweet pepper strips. In some countries, the *tamal* is wrapped in a corn husk. Here in Costa Rica banana or plantain leaves are utilized.

Making tamales can be a major task, so we suggest you gather a few friends and have a tamale making day! Tamales will stay fresh for a couple of weeks and make great holiday treats to give to friends and neighbors.

CHRISTMAS TAMALES
Tamales Navideños

1 lb. pork ribs
2 lbs. lean pork shoulder
  or chicken
3 lbs. masa
2 lbs. potatoes
1 lb. lard, melted
1 1/2 green olives
1 cup raisins
2 green peppers, julienned

1 med. large onion
1 bunch parsley, chopped
1 bunch cilantro, chopped
salt and pepper to taste
1 tsp.oregano leaves, crushed
1/4 cup achiote mix or to
    to taste (Los Patitos brand)
1 small can of peas
10 cloves of garlic, crushed

4 lbs. clean banana leaves to wrap the tamales
String to tie

Cook the chicken or pork along with the pork ribs in water to cover. Add the onion cut in quarters, the crushed garlic cloves, the chopped parsley, the chopped cilantro, and the oregano. Cook until tender, then remove from the liquid, drain, and cut the meats into small pieces.

Peel and cut the potatoes, then boil, drain, and mash while hot. Mix the masa with 6-8 cups of strained broth from the meats. Add salt to taste. Add the mashed potatoes. Mix in the melted lard. Save 1/2 cup of this mixture.

Melt 1/2 cup of the achiote paste in a frying pan. Add a tsp. of oregano, pepper to taste, and then add the reserved masa mixture. Remove from the heat.

To form the tamales, insert into a ball of the masa, 1 tsp. achiote mixture, pieces of the meat, one pea, two olives, two bell pepper strips, and two raisins. Shape the ball into an oblong square and place lengthwise on a banana leaf. Fold the ends toward the center. Stack two tamales together to form a "piña", then tie them together with a string.

Put several "piñas" in a large stovetop pot lined with banana leaves. Add cold water to cover. Put a lid on the pot and cook the tamales, once the water comes to a boil, for about 1 1/2 hours over a low heat.

The tamales can be eaten right away or cooled and refrigerated or frozen for later use. Refrigerated they will last 4 or 5 days. They can be frozen for several weeks, then reheated in a microwave!!

Makes: about 40

COSTA RICAN RICE AND BEANS...

Gallo Pinto, literally speckled rooster, has its origin in Nicaragua, but it is the national dish of Costa Rica! It's found thoughout Central America and the Caribbean. In Cuba this rice and bean dish is called *moros y cristianos* while in El Salvador it is called *casamiento*. Ticos serve *gallo pinto* on breakfast plates and with lunch or dinner. The following recipe is one made by Flor, an employee in Carolina's store.

FLOR'S GALLO PINTO
Gallo Pinto de Flor

1 1/2 cups cold firm cooked black beans (pg 144)
2 1/2 cups cold cooked rice
1/2 cup bean broth
1 medium onion, minced
1 T. Salsa Lizano

1 green bell pepper, finely chopped
1 garlic clove, minced
1/2 cup chopped cilantro, or to taste
2 T. vegetable oil

In a large skillet, heat the vegetable oil, then add the onion and garlic. Sauté until crystalized. Add the green pepper and sauté for 2 additional minutes. Add the beans, broth, and the Salsa Lizano. Simmer for 10 minutes. Add the rice and cilantro, mixing well. Cover and cook for 5 to 10 minutes, frequently stiring to make sure the mixture is throughly heated.

Serve with tortillas and sour cream. For a hearty breakfast, serve eggs, any style, with *gallo pinto* and bacon on the side.

Serves: 4

TICO BURRITOS...

When Marilyn was confined to bed with a back problem, a Costa Rican neighbor prepared these "burritos" and brought them to her to enjoy. Just as "tacos" in Costa Rica are very dissimilar to those found in the States and Mexico, these are not burritos in the sense which North Americans know them. They are fried in oil and are akin to Mexican chimichangas.

166

TINA'S TICO "BURRITOS"
Burritos de Tina

1 package flour tortillas
2 chicken breasts, boneless
  and skinless
1 lb. Turrialba or Monterey
  Jack cheese, grated
1 lb. refried beans
Salsa Lizano

2 tomatoes, chopped
1/2 cup tomato sauce
1/2 cup chopped onion
1 celery rib, minced
1/2 green pepper, chopped
1 garlic clove, minced
1/2 cup water

Cook the chicken with the chopped tomato, celery rib, and garlic in 1 cup of water. Simmer for about 20 minutes or until done. Remove the chicken from the broth and chop.

Sauté the onion and pepper. Add the tomato sauce and 1/2 cup water, then the chicken pieces and chicken mixture. Simmer for 15 minutes.

Heat the tortillas until soft. Spread the refried beans on top, then the grated cheese. Sprinkle with the chicken mixture. Roll up like a taco, folding the ends under, and fry in hot oil until golden.

Serve with toppings of your choice: chopped lettuce, chopped tomato, guacamole, sour cream, etc.

Makes: 8 to 10

SALVADOREAN PUPUSAS...

Since Carolina is Salvadorean our guide would be incomplete without including a few of her favorites. *Pupuserías, pupusa* snack places, can be found throughout El Salvador; it seems like on almost every block. In late afternoon their fires are flaring and their griddles are hot as Salvadorians stop to eat one or more of these little stuffed pancakes.

Pupusas are made with *masa* dough and can be filled with a variety of ingredients; the usual ones are beans and cheese, pork and tomato, or combinations of these items. Lately, you can find Salvadorians enjoying more exotic fillings like mushrooms and cheese, shrimp, chicken curry, and jalapeños and cheese. The sky is the limit! You may want to add some of these to the cheese in our recipe. Since the cheese and bean *pupusa* is very "*tipico*", you can make these pupusas by adding a half cup of stiff cold refried beans to our basic recipe.

Pupusas are usually served accompanied by a cabbage relish, *curtido*. In addition to being an afternoon snack food, they are served as hors d'oeuvres at special parties and celebrations.

CHEESE PUPUSAS
Pupusas de Queso

2 cups masa flour (Masa Rica)   1/4 lb. Jack or Turrialba or
1 sm. pkg. (3 oz.) cream cheese   other white cheese
6 oz. parmesan or cotija cheese

In a bowl, stir the masa with a fork, gradually adding 1 1/4 cups water until moistened and the dough holds together.

As you shape pupusas, you need to moisten your hands frequently, so have a bowl of water available. Moisten hands; shape dough into 12 equal balls and cover.

Cut the jack cheese, cream cheese, and parmesan cheese into chunks. Whirl smooth in a food processor. (Or finely shred the jack and grate the parmesan. Stir with cream cheese until well mixed.) Moisten hands and shape cheese mixture into 12 equal balls and cover.

Pat 1 ball of masa between moistened hands to make a 4-inch round. Put 1 cheese ball in center; fold masa around cheese. Roll ball in palms to smoothly seal in cheese. Pat between palms to make a smooth 4-inch round; if masa cracks, moisten to smooth. If cheese breaks through, cover with a pinch of masa. If making ahead, stack pupusas with pieces of plastic wrap between them. Seal in a plastic bag and chill up to 1 day.

Place a non stick griddle or 2 non stick frying pans, each 10 to 12 inches, over medium heat. (Or heat an electric griddle or frying pan to 350°F.) When griddle is hot, lay pupusas slightly apart on it. Cook until brown on the bottom; turn, and brown the other side, 8 to 12 minutes total. Serve hot or keep warm until all are cooked.

Makes: 12,   4 to 6 servings

Curtido...

3 cups shredded green cabbage   1 dried bay leaf
1/3 cup chopped onion   1 sm. carrot (about 2 oz.), cut
1/2 tsp. dried oregano   diagonally into thin slices
1/3 cup white wine vinegar   Salt (optional)
1 fresh hot pepper, such as a jalapeño or Fresno, stemmed and
    minced (optional)

168

Mix cabbage, oregano, onion, and hot pepper. Put in a tall 1-quart glass or plastic container. Tuck the bay leaf and carrot slices between glass and cabbage mixture.

Mix vinegar, 1 tsp. salt (if desired), and 1 3/4 cups of water. Pour over vegetables, cover, and chill at least 4 hours or up to one week . Serve with a slotted spoon.

Makes: about 3 1/2 cups

SALVADORIAN SALPICON...

Salpicón, a cold beef salad, is most typically served for lunch on hot summer days in El Salvador. Salvadorians usually prepare white rice and homemade tortillas to accompany their *salpicón*.

SALVADORIAN COLD BEEF SALAD
Salpicón

Meat preparation:

1 lb. beef chuck	2 sprigs parsley
1 onion, quartered	2 sprigs cilantro
2 garlic cloves	Salt and pepper

Mixture ingredients:

1/2 cup chopped peppermint	1/4 cup lime juice
4 T. chopped parsley	Salt and pepper to taste
3/4 cup minced onion	2 T. chopped spearmint

In a large pot, cover the beef with water and boil with all the meat preparation ingredients for about 1 1/2 to 2 hours, until very tender. Cool the meat in its broth, then remove it from the pot and finely chop it with a knife or meat cleaver.

Mix the cool meat with the mixture ingredients listed above and refrigerate.

Serves: 4

NICARAGUAN PASTELITOS...

The Nicaraguans make *pastelitos*, tiny meat pies, which are served at most social events: birthdays, communions, and anniversaries. These meat filled pastries are traditionally dusted with sugar after frying!

NICARAGUAN MEAT PIES
Pastelitos de Nicaragua

Dough:

1/2 cup solid veg. shortening

2 cups all-purpose flour

3/4 tsp. salt

1/2 cup warm water

Filling:

6 oz. boneless, skinless chicken
 breast or pork, diced

1/2 tomato, peeled, seeded,
 and finely chopped

1/2 green bell pepper, cored,
 seeded, and minced

1/2 rib celery, minced

1 T. tomato paste

Salt and Pepper to taste

1 1/2 T. dried currants

4 pitted green olives, chopped

About 1 cup of water

1 to 2 T. fine, dried bread
 crumbs (optional)

About 2 cups of vegetable oil for frying.
About 1/2 cup of granulated sugar for dusting.

Prepare the dough: Cut up the shortening and put with salt into the flour, using two knives or a food processor. Add enough water to make a soft pliable dough. Wrap the dough in plastic and let it rest at room temperature for 2 hours.

Prepare the filling: Combine the chicken, tomato, onion, bell pepper celery, tomato paste, and salt and pepper in a large saucepan. Add enough water just to cover. Gently simmer the mixture until the chicken is tender, about 20 minutes. Drain the filling in a colander, reserving the cooking liquid.

Coarsely chop the filling in a food processor to the consistency of ground beef. Stir in the currants, olives, and salt and pepper to taste. If the mixture is too dry, add a little of the reserved cooking liquid. If it's too runny, stir in the bread crumbs.

170

On a lightly floured surface, roll out half of the dough as thin as possible. Cut out 2-inch circles, using a cookie cutter. Roll out the remaining dough and cut out 1 3/4 inch circles. Gather up the scraps into a ball, roll out and cut, until all of the dough is used.

Assemble the pastelitos: Brush the smaller dough circles with water and place a small spoonful of filling in the center of each. Place the larger circle on top. Seal the dough circles by crimping the edges with a fork. (The *pastelitos* can be prepared ahead to this stage and frozen.)

Just before serving, pour the oil to a depth of 1 inch in a heavy skillet or frying pan and heat to 350°F. Fry the *pastelitos* until golden brown on both sides, 2 to 3 minutes total. Work in several batches so as not to crowd the pan. Drain the *pastelitos* on paper towels. Lightly sprinkle the *pastelitos* with the sugar and serve at once.

Note: For a healthier, although less succulent version, the *pastelitos* can be baked instead of fried. Brush with a beaten egg, sprinkle lightly with sugar, and bake in a preheated 400°F oven until golden brown, about 20 minutes.

Makes: 40

NICARAGUAN CARNE EN VAHO...

This steamed beef and vegetable dish is typically served as a casual meal on a lazy Sunday or on a country weekend. The meal is prepared for family, friends, and neighbors to share....Try it. It's fun to prepare for a large group!

NICARAGUAN STEAMED BEEF
Carne en Vaho

Marinade:
3 lbs. skirt steak   6 garlic cloves, chopped
Juice from 4 sour oranges, approx. 1 cup
    (or 1/2 cup lime juice and 1/2 cup orange juice)

Dish ingredients:
3 ripe plantains   3 large tomatoes
3 medium yucas   4 green peppers, cut in rings
2 medium onions, sliced

Pot preparation:
3 small sticks of wood

4 banana leaves

Accompanying Salad:
1 head cabbage, shredded as
    for cole slaw
3 large tomatoes, chopped

1/4 cup vinegar
Salt to taste

    The evening before serving, prepare a marinade with the chopped garlic, lime/orange juice or sour orange juice. Put the meat in a pyrex baking dish and add the sliced onions, chopped tomatoes, and salt. Pour the garlic and juice marinade over the ingredients, baste well, cover, and refrigerate overnight. Turn the meat occasionally while marinating.

    Into a large pot, pour 3 cups of water. On the bottom of the pot, put the 3 sticks of wood and line the pot with the banana leaves to form a bed. Leave a banana leaf to drape over the dish later.

    Peel and cut the yuca into 3 sections and place it on the layer of banana leaves.   Peel the plantains and place them on top of the yuca. Place the beef along with its marinade, tomatoes, and onions on top. Cover the ingredients with banana leaves and put a heavy lid on the pot so the steam will not escape. Bring to a boil and simmer for about 3 hours.

    Serve with the cabbage salad accompanied by fresh cheese on the side.

    Serves: 6

HONDURAN FLOUR TORTILLAS WITH TOPPINGS...

Carolina and her friends love to be invited to Lorena's for breakfast because she and her maid usually prepare *baleadas*. These little grilled tortillas are covered with beans and sprinkled with sour cream and parmesan cheese, then folded to make tasty small morsels. *Baleadas* are principally served at breakfast, but can also be eaten as an appetizer or a snack.   Serve them with a good cup of Costa Rican coffee--Sunburst Brand, of course!

HONDURAN BALEADAS
Baleadas de Honduras

4 cups flour   1 tsp. salt
1 tsp. baking powder   1 cup water
1/4 cup vegetable shortening
2 cups mashed refried beans--canned or prepared to your taste.

In a bowl, sift the flour with the baking powder and salt. Mix in the shortening to form a course meal.   Add water, little by little, to form a large ball.

Knead the dough until it is elastic and does not stick to your hands. Form 2 inch balls. Let them rest for 10 to 20 minutes.

Heat a lightly greased heavy skillet.   Start making the tortillas by streching each ball between two sheets of wax paper, either by hand or using a rolliing pin. Form rounds 4-inches in diameter. Cook each on both sides, about 2 minutes per side, until the tortilla puffs.

Heat up the refried beans. Spread about 1 tablespoon on each fried tortilla. Top the beans with parmesasn cheese and sour cream, then fold..

Makes: 8 to 10

HONDURAN YUCA WITH PORK RINDS...

This dish, a favorite of a Honduran friend, is consumed throughout Central America. It is tipically served as a late afternoon snack or as a light lunch entree. It goes great with an iced cold beer!

YUCA WITH PORK RINDS
Yuca con Chicharrones

1 1/2 lbs. peeled yuca   1/3 cup lime juice
1/2 tsp. salt   2 green bell peppers, finely
3 1/2 cups cabbage,   chopped
   finely shredded   2 medium tomatoes, chopped
1 medium onion, thinly sliced   1/2 lb. chicharrones (Fried
1/4 cup white wine vinegar   Pork Rinds), warmed and
                                                      broken into pieces

In a sauce pan, combine the yuca with salt and enough water to cover. Bring to a boil, lower the heat, and cook for about 20 minutes or until fork tender. Drain and cover.

In a mixing bowl, mix the cabbage and onion with the vinegar and the lime juice. Add the green bell pepper, toss, and marinate for at least 30 minutes. Mix in the chopped tomatoes just before serving.

Line a pyrex dish with the yuca. Sprinkle with a little salt. Cover with the cabbage salad and top with the fried pork rinds.

Serves: 6

GUATEMALAN CHURRASCO...

 *Churrasco* is the Argentinean word for grilled beef. Costa Rica, Nicaragua, and Honduras are the principal beef producing countries in Central America. They import beef to Guatemala where *churrasco* is very popular. *Churrasco* is most typically served with three sauces: *chimichurri*, a spicy tomato salsa, and a pickled onion relish, but you can utilize any of our guide's salsas or prepare your favorites.

GUATEMALAN GRILLED BEEF
Churrasco de Guatemala

1 piece beef tenderloin (about 2 1/2 lbs.), trimmed of fat and veins

Marinade:

1/2 cup chopped cilantro	3 T. sherry vinegar or wine
3 cloves garlic, minced	vinegar
1/4 cup olive oil	1 tsp. ground white pepper
1/4 cup dry sherry	1 tsp. salt

Cut the tenderloin lengthwise, with the grain, into 4 flat, even strips. Place the strips between sheets of plastic wrap and gently pound with the side of a cleaver to form steaks about 10 inches long and 1/2 inch thick.

Combine all of the marinade ingredients in a nonreactive dish or bowl. Add the beef and marinate, covered in the refrigerator for 1 to 2 hours, turning occasionally.

174

Preheat a barbecue grill to very hot or preheat the broiler with the tray 3 inches from the heat.

Drain the beef and blot dry with paper towels. Grill or broil the beef for 1 minute per side for rare; 1 to 1 1/2 minutes per side for medium; and 2 minutes per side for well done.

Serves: 4

GUATEMALAN STUFFED CHILE PEPPERS...

Chiles Rellenos are familiar to most North Americans. Although often associated with Mexico, they are a favorite throughout Central America. Each country has its varations...Some like them hot; others prefer a blander dish. You can use whatever type of chile you want. Fillings can vary as well. *Chiles Rellenos* can be stuffed with just about anything, but the usual ingredients are pork, beef, or cheese. Our recipe for *Chiles Rellenos* is a Guatemalan version.

STUFFED PEPPERS
Chiles Rellenos

12 green bell peppers,
    roasted and peeled
1 lb. pork shoulder or chicken,
    cooked in 4 cups of water

2 tsp. salt
1 onion, quartered
1 celery rib, sliced

Add all the ingredients to 4 cups of water. When the meat is cooked, drain it and discard the liquid, onion and celery. Let the meat cool, then mince it finely and mix it with:

1/2 cup finely chopped carrot   1/2 cup minced green beans

Simmer the mixture in 1/2 cup of water for about 15 minutes.

3 T. cooking oil   2 T. finely minced onion
1 finely chopped garlic clove

Meanwhile sauté in cooking oil minced onion and garlic. When chrystalized, add the meat mixture and the following:

2 T. bread crumbs	2 T. vinegar or cooking wine
1/2 tsp. ground pepper	1 tsp. salt
1/4 tsp. ground nutmeg	1/2 cup raisins (optional)

Let the mixture cool.

| 4 egg whites and 4 egg yolks | 1/2 cup cooking oil |

Whip stiff 4 egg whites. When stiff blend in the 4 egg yolks., one at a time. Stuff the chiles with the meat mixture. Dip them into the egg mixture. Using a heavy skillet. fry the chiles in hot oil.

Serve with rice and if you desire a fresh tomato sauce.

Makes: 12 stuffed chiles, serving 4 to 6

PANAMENIAN SHORT RIBS AND VEGETABLE STEW...

This Panamenian favorite, with influences from both the north and the south, reflects Panama's location as a bridge between two continents. The stew utilizes vegetables and tubers native to Latin America and has a unique taste.

PANAMENIAN SHORT RIBS AND VEGETABLE STEW
Estofado de Panama

2 lbs. beef short ribs, cut into 2-inch lengths, fat trimmed	1 tsp. dired oregano leaves
2 quarts regular strength beef or chicken broth	1 large green plantain, cut into 1-inch lengths
4 cloves garlic, crushed	1 lb. fresh yuca, peeled and cut into 1-inch lengths
1 large onion, cut into 1-inch chunks	1 lb. (2 large ears) corn, each ear cut into 4 equal pieces
2 medium tomatoes, cored and thinly sliced	1 lb. ñampi (about 3 med. sized)
1 medium green pepper, stemed, seeded, and sliced	1/2 cup cilantro, chopped

Rinse the meat and put into a 6 to 8 quart pan. Add the broth, garlic, onions, tomatoes, bell pepper, cilantro, and oregano. Bring to a boil over a high heat. Reduce the heat and simmer for about two hours.

Prepare the plantain, yuca, ñampi, and corn. Add all except the ñampi. Simmer covered for about 15 minutes. Then add the ñampi and simmer 20 to 30 minutes longer, until the meat and vegetables are tender when pierced. Skim and discard the fat.

Before serving, salt and pepper to taste, and garnish portions with chopped cilantro. Serve with rice.

Serves: 8

CENTRAL AMERICAN ROPA VIEJA...

 *Ropa Vieja* translates as "old clothes". No one quite knows how this stew acquired its name, but most likely from the shredded appearance of the dish's meat. It originated in Cuba, but can be found throughout Central America. *Ropa Vieja* is traditionally served with white rice and *maduros*.

"OLD CLOTHES" STEW
Ropa Vieja

For braising the beef:
1 1/2 lbs. skirt steak or flank steak
1 small onion, quartered
1 carrot, cut into 1-inch pieces

1 tomato, quartered
2 cloves garlic, peeled

To finish the dish:
2 T. olive oil
2 cloves garlic, minced
1 small onion, thinly sliced
1/2 green pepper, cored, seeded, and thinly sliced
1/2 red pepper, cored, seeded, and thinly sliced

1/2 tsp. ground cumin, or to taste
1/3 cup tomato purée
3 T. dry white wine
salt and freshly ground black pepper, to taste

Combine the beef, quartered onion, tomato, carrot, and garlic cloves with 6 cups water in a large pot. Bring to a boil over a high heat. Skim off the scum that rises to the surface. Reduce the heat and simmer the beef, uncovered, skimming often, until tender, 40 to 50 minutes.

Strain the meat, reserving the broth for a soup. (Just add rice, lentils, or cooked beans and throw in a few vegetables.) Let the meat cool. Tear it, along the grain, into pencil-thin strips.

Heat the oil in a large nonreactive frying pan over medium heat. Add the minced garlic, sliced onion, and bell pepper strips. Cook until soft but not brown, 3 to 4 minutes. Stir in the meat, cumin, tomato purée, wine, salt and pepper. Cook until the meat is well coated with the sauce and the sauce is reduced and flavorful, about 5 minutes. Correct the seasonings, adding salt and pepper to taste.

Serves: 4

CLASSIC CENTRAL AMERICAN SWEETS

 Latins definitely have a sweet tooth! For many Central Americans it is an afternoon ritual to have a cup of coffee, *cafecito*, and a "sweet", *dulce*. Is this the Hispanic equivalent of British "tea time"? The late afternoon respite is the traditional way to relax and unwind after working either at home or at one's business since the early hours. Ties with family and friends are strong in Central American culture, so this is a time gather to share family news, events of the day, and local gossip.

We offer here some "classic" Central American desserts for you to sample. While living or visiting here, you may want to take up this afternoon ritual!

QUESADILLAS SALVADORENAS...

Quesadillas Salvadoreñas are small tea cakes served in El Salvador warm out of the oven with coffee as a mid-morning or late afternoon nourishment.

SALVADORIAN TEA CAKES
Quesadillas Salvadorenas

1 cup milk
1 cup sour cream
2 cups sugar
4 eggs
1 cup grated parmesan cheese

2 cups bisquick or Aunt
    Jemima pancake mix
2 sticks butter, melted
4 T. toasted sesame seeds

Mix with a fork the milk, sour cream, sugar, and eggs. Melt the butter, let it cool, then add it to the liquid ingredients.

With a blender at a slow speed, blend the pancake mix into the liquid ingredients. Add the grated parmesan cheese.

Pour the mixture into a greased 9 x 12 pyrex baking dish or a muffin pan. Top with the sesame seeds, and bake at 350°F for 30 minutes.

Makes: 12 portions

TRES LECHES...

This desert is a Costa Rican favorite. Its origin is in Nicaragua, but it is savored throughout Central America and México. Three different kinds of milk are used to prepare *Tres Leches* (Three Milks): fresh milk, evaporated milk, and sweetened condensed milk. The best of these desserts are very moist.

THREE MILK CAKE
Tres Leches

Cake:

1 cup sugar
5 large eggs, separated
1/3 cup milk
1/2 tsp. vanilla extract

1 cup all-purpose flour
1 1/2 tsp. baking powder
1/2 tsp. cream of tartar

Milk Syrup:

1 can (12 oz.) evaporated milk
1 cup sweetened condensed milk
1 cup heavy (or whipping) cream

1 tsp. vanilla extract
1 T. light rum

Meringue:

1 cup sugar
1/2 tsp. cream of tartar

3 egg whites

Preheat the oven to 350°F. Generously butter a 13 x 9 inch baking dish.

Prepare the cake: Beat 3/4 cup of the sugar and the egg yolks until light and fluffy, about 5 minutes. Fold in the milk, vanilla, flour, and baking powder.

Beat the egg whites to soft peaks, adding the cream of tartar after 20 seconds. Gradually add the remaining 1/4 cup sugar and continue beating until the whites are glossy and firm, but not dry. Gently fold the whites into the yolk mixture. Pour this batter into the buttered baking dish.

Bake the cake until it feels firm and an inserted toothpick comes out clean, 40 to 50 minutes. Let the cake cool completely on a wire rack. Unmold the cake onto a large, deep platter. Pierce the cake all over with a fork.

Prepare the milk syrup: Combine the evaporated milk, sweetened condensed milk, cream, vanilla, and rum in a mixing bowl. Whisk until well mixed. Pour the syrup over the cake, spooning the overflow back on top until all is absorbed.

Prepare the meringue: Place 3/4 cup plus 2 tablespoons of sugar in a heavy saucepan with 1/4 cup water. Cover and cook over high heat for 2 minutes. Uncover the pan and cook the sugar to the soft ball stage, 239°F on a candy thermometer, 6 to 8 minutes.

Meanwhile, beat the egg whites to soft peaks with the cream of tartar. Add the remaining 2 tablespoons sugar and continue beating to stiff peaks. Pour the boiling sugar syrup in a thin stream into the whites and continue beating until the mixture is cool to the touch. The hot syrup "cooks" the whites.

Using a wet spatula, spread over the top of the cake a thick layer of meringue. Refrigerate the cake for at least 2 hours before serving.

Serves: 8 to 10

ARROZ CON LECHE...

Rice with milk, *arroz con leche*, is a popular dessert in just about every Central American country. It's a creamy pudding not unlike some of those rice puddings our mothers made for us when we were kids.

RICE PUDDING
Arroz con Leche

1 cup short-grain rice
1 cinnamon stick (2 inches long)
3 strips lemon zest
1 vanilla bean, split
1 can (12 oz.) evaporated milk
1 can (14 oz,) sweetened
  condensed milk

1/2 cup raisins, soaked in
  warm water to cover
1/2 cup pine nuts, lightly
  toasted (optional)
1 to 2 T. sugar, or to taste
ground cinnamon or freshly
  grated nutmeg

Wash the rice several times until the water runs clear. Put the rice in a large heavy sauce pan, add 2 1/2 cups of fresh water, the cinnamon stick, the lemon zest, and the vanilla bean. Bring to a boil over a high heat. Reduce the heat, cover, and gently simmer until the rice absorbs the water, about 20 minutes.

Stir in the evaporated milk. Gently simmer, uncovered, until most of the liquid is absorbed, about 8 minutes.   Stir occasionally.

Stir in the sweetened condensed milk, the raisins, and the pine nuts, if using. Gently simmer, uncovered, until most of the liquid is absorbed and the rice is very tender, about 6 minutes. The pudding should remain very moist. Stir occasionally.

Remove the cinnamon stick, lemon zest, and vanilla bean. Stir in the sugar, to taste. Transfer to a bowl and let the rice pudding cool to room temperature.

To serve, transfer the pudding to a serving bowl or individual bowls. Sprinkle with the ground cinnamon and serve at once.

Serves: 8

FLAN...

Flan is a custard dessert prepared in most Spanish speaking countries. It has many variations. It can be prepared individually in small round molds or cut in pieces from a large loaf pan. Its texture can range from very smooth to rather coarse. The basic ingredients are always the same, but coconut can be added and seasonings can change according to the whim of the cook. A rich caramel sauce which sometimes included brandy or other liquors always tops flan.

CARAMEL CUSTARD
Flan

1 1/2 cups sugar
3 large whole eggs
1 egg yolk
2 cups milk

1 1/2 T. Spanish brandy
1 tsp. vanilla extract
1/2 tsp. ground cinnamon,
    or to taste

Preheat the oven to 350°F. Have ready six 8-ounce ramekins.

Make the caramel: Place 1 cup of the sugar in a heavy saucepan with 3 tablespoons water. Cover and cook the sugar over high heat for 1 minute. Uncover the pan and continue cooking until the mixture turns dark golden brown, about 4 minutes.

Pour a little of this mixture into each ramekin. Tilt and rotate the ramekins to coat the bottom and sides. Set aside.

Meanwhile, bring 1 quart of water to a boil.

Whisk together the remaining 1/2 cup sugar, the whole eggs, and egg yolk in a mixing bowl. Whisk in the milk, brandy, vanilla, and cinnamon. Correct the flavors, adding sugar or cinnamon to taste. Pour this mixture into the ramekins.

Place the ramekins in a small roasting pan and pour in boiling water to a depth of 1/2 inch. Loosely cover the pan with aluminum foil. Bake until the flan puffs slightly and an inserted skewer comes out clean, about 20 minutes.

182

Remove the flan from the roasting pan, and let cool to room temperature. Cover and refrigerate until cold, at least 6 hours. The flan sets even better if you allow it to chill overnight. Just before serving, run a sharp knife around the inside of each ramekin. Place a plate on the top and invert. Gently shake the dish. The flan should slip out easily. Spoon the caramel sauce over the flan and serve.

Serves: 6

CARDENAL...

Carolina swears her Aunt Violeta and Aunt Gloria are just about the best cooks in El Salvador. She says her Aunt Violeta's *Cardenal* is "to die for"! It's a special favorite in the Avila family. The *Cardenal* is a light and airy dessert prepared to celebrate a special birthday or an important event. It is fairly easy to make, beautiful to look at, and delicious to eat.

AUNT VIOLETA'S CARDENAL CAKE
Cardenal de Tia Violeta

1 cup of egg whites, about 8 eggs	1 tsp. vanilla
2 cups refined sugar	1/2 teaspoon salt
2 T. cornstarch	1 tsp. cream of tartar

Filling:

2 cups whipping cream	1 pint of strawberries, sliced
1/2 cup fine sugar	in half or sliced canned
1 tsp. vanilla	peaches

Beat the egg whites with the cream of tartar until they form peaks. Add 2 cups sugar, one tablespoon at a time and continue beating. Then add the cornstarch and vanilla, beating until the egg whites are stiff, but not dry.

Preheat the oven to 225°F. Cover the bottom of two round 9-inch cake pans with waxed paper or greased aluminum foil. Divide the egg white mixture between the two pans. Bake for 2 hours. Leave the mixture in the oven to dry for 8 hours or overnight.

To make the filling, beat the whipping cream with the sugar. Remove the contents from one 9-inch cake pan and place on a platter. Put half of the whipped cream and half of the strawberries on top. Add the remaining cake pan contents and

top with the leftover whipped cream and strawberries. Refrigerate for 3 hours before serving.
Serves: 10

BUDIN DE PAN...

Bread pudding is very popular in Costa Rica. When Carolina owned Café El Sol, she found her *budín de pan* to be a hit with both visitors and locals alike.

CAROLINA'S BREAD PUDDING
Budín de Pan de Carolina

1 (2 lb.) loaf of sliced white
   bread, crusts removed
1/2 cup butter, softened
1/2 cup raisins
1/3 cup rum
2 1/2 cups milk

2 1/2 cups whipping
   cream
2 tsp. vanilla
8 eggs
1 cup sugar
1/4 cup cinnamon sugar

Carmel Sauce:
1 1/2 cups sugar
1/2 cup water
1/2 cup butter

1 1/2 cups whipping
   cream
1/4 cup rum

Spread some soft butter on to the bread slices. Toast lightly on one side only. Cut the bread into 1/2 inch squares. Set aside.

Put the raisins in the rum to soak and soften. Set aside.

Mix the milk and whipping cream. Add the vanilla and set aside.

Beat the eggs with the sugar, then add to the milk mixture. Stir in the bread cubes and the raisin mixture. Let stand for 20 minutes.

Pour into a well buttered 9 x 13 glass baking dish. Dot with the remaining butter and sprinkle with cinnamon sugar. Bake at 325°F for 45 to 60 minutes, until light brown on the top.

Serve with the carmel sauce.
Serves: 8

Carmel sauce:

In a sauce pan, melt the sugar in water over a low heat until carmelized. Add the butter and 1 1/2 cups of whipping cream. Simmer until desired consistency. Pour warm over the bread pudding.

COFFEE IS KING!

If the banana is the queen of Central American food products, coffee must be the king! The plant from whose "beans" we make coffee is indigenous to Ethiopia and the Sudan. The term "coffee" most likely is derived from the the Ethiopian name, *kaffa*. The practice of infusing ground roasted coffee beans in water appears to have begun in 15th century Arabia. (The world's first coffee house opened in Mecca around 1511!) From Arabia coffee drinking spread to Turkey and finally to Europe and Great Britain in the mid-17th century.

The coffee "tree" is actually an evergreen shrub. It grows best in hot, moist climates. The most flavorful beans are produced at elevations between 3,000 and 6,000 feet, making the Latin American and Central American highlands prime areas for the production of this commodity. Of the many varieties of the genus *Coffea*, family Rubiaceae, only two species have significant commercial importance: *C. arabica* and *C. robusta*. Together they constitute 99 percent of the world's total coffee output. *Coffea robusta* is a sturdy, disease-resistsant species which thrives at lower altitudes and produces beans with a harsher flavor than the more sensitive *coffea arabica*. Coffee lovers prefer the latter because it has a more elegant aroma and flavor..

Every coffee drinker has been introduced to the rich, flavorful Colombian coffees by their advertising spokesperson, Juan Valdez. Most Americans are familiar with the mild, sweet, full-bodied Kona coffee from Hawaii. In the last several decades, Costa Rican coffee has emerged as a favored product in the North American and European markets. Noted for its bouquet, Costa Rican coffee is often added to "blends" to provide a captivating aroma.

Coffee is grown on both the Atlantic and Pacific slopes of the Costa Rican central plateau, *Meseta Central*. All coffees produced in Costa Rica are of the *Coffea arabica* genus. Believe it or not there are more than 30,000 coffee farms in Costa Rica, however, most are under 85 acres in size.

Coffee "cherries", so called for their shape and color, are harvested by hand and transported from the fields to coffee mills where the pulp is removed from the bean by a dry or wet separation process. When the coffee beans have been thoroughly dried, they are sorted, bagged, graded, and shipped to processors. Unprocessed beans are an unappealing gray-green color. It is only after roasting they change to their rich brown color and develop their distinctive flavor and aroma. Many beans are exported for roasting elsewhere, but many coffees are roasted right here in Costa Rica by both big and small producers. An interesting experience is to visit a coffee roasting facility...like Sunburst in Escazú!

The Costa Rican government, as well as the governments of most other coffee producing countries, controls the coffee industry. New plantings are limited to keep coffee the "king" with stable prices and superior quality.

When purchasing coffee, it is best to pay a little more and buy coffee made for export. It will be of the finest quality and a steal compared to what coffee of comparable quality costs outside of Central America. Some coffees prepared for local consumption are laced with sugar and other items which will not appeal to coffee purists! To meet foreign demand, local coffee makers are now making some decaf coffees, but they inform us this is not "real" coffee. Decaffeinating, in their opinion, takes the "essence" away from coffee.

The length of time coffee beans are roasted will affect the color and flavor of the brew. In general, dark roasts, like French roasts and the Italian or espresso roasts, are stronger and smoother than light roasts. The coffee known as American roast is also called regular roast because the beans are medium-roasted, which results in a brew not too light nor too heavy. Some interesting blends are now available in Costa Rica where macadamia and chocolate flavorings, among others, have been added. Look for these types under the Sunburst label.

Coffee, whether ground or whole-bean, loses its flavor quickly. To assure the freshest, most flavorful coffee, one needs to purchase fresh beans and grind only as many beans as needed to brew a pot. Ideally when brewing coffee one should use freshly drawn, soft water. Carefully time your coffee maker, and never boil your coffee!! Boiling brings out the tannic acid and can make the coffee brew bitter and cloudy. The old office method of brewing the coffee in the morning and keeping it warm most of the day is convenient, but produces terrible coffee!

You can store whole roasted beans (*granos*) in an airtight container in a cool, dry place for up to 2 weeks. For longer storage, the beans can be frozen, but should be used within 2 months. Once a package is opened, ground coffee (*café molido*) begins to go stale in a couple of days at room-temperature. It should should be refrigerated in an airtight container and used within two weeks.

It's no wonder the Costa Rican's call the coffee bean, *grano de oro*, for it is definitely pure "gold"!

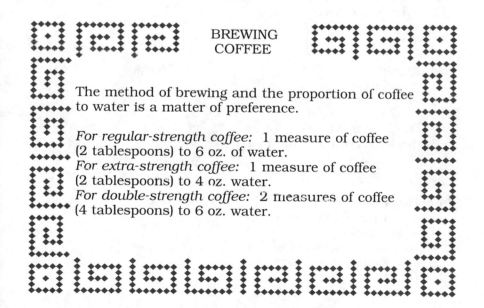

BREWING COFFEE

The method of brewing and the proportion of coffee to water is a matter of preference.

For regular-strength coffee: 1 measure of coffee (2 tablespoons) to 6 oz. of water.
For extra-strength coffee: 1 measure of coffee (2 tablespoons) to 4 oz. water.
For double-strength coffee: 2 measures of coffee (4 tablespoons) to 6 oz. water.

COFFEE DRINKS

HOT COFFEES

Beso Brujo   Serves 1
    8 oz. hot freshly brewed coffee
    1 oz. Café Rica (Costa Rican brand liquor)
        or Khalua

Mexican Coffee   Serves 1
    8 oz. hot freshly brewed coffee
    1 cinnamon stick to stir
    2 tablespoon whipped cream
    1 teaspoon powdered chocolate

Café Borgia   Serves 1
    4 oz. hot freshly brewed coffee
    4 oz. hot chocolate
    Twist of orange rind
    2 tablespoons whipped cream
    Sprinkle of ground cinnamon

Chocolaccino   Serves 1
    4 oz. hot freshly brewed coffee
    4 oz. hot milk
    3 tablespoons whipped cream
    2 tablespoons chocolate curls

COLD COFFEES

Marilyn's Chilled Coffee
Serves: 6 to 8

6 heaping tablespoons espresso
2 cups water
3 level tablespoons sugar, or to taste
3 to 3 1/2 cups milk
1 tablespoon liquid cinnamon (*Doña Petra Canela*)

Brew the espresso in 2 cups water. Pour into bowl containing the sugar, stir well, and let cool. Add the milk to the coffee mixture and approximately 1 tablespoon liquid cinnamon to flavor. Chill in a pitcher in the refrigerator.

Mocha Frost
Serves 1

4 oz. cold coffee
6 oz. chocolate ice cream
6 oz. vanilla ice cream
Dash of nutmeg

Mix all the ingredients in a blender. Serve in a goblet or tall glass.

Espresso Batido
Serves 1

8 oz. very strong cold espresso
Sugar to taste
1/2 cup cracked ice

Whirl in a blender until smooth. Serve immediately.

The Kick
Serves 1

1/2 cup espresso
1 teaspoon super fine sugar
2 tablespoons rum
1 tablespoon Café Rica
2 tablespoons heavy cream

Dissolve the sugar in the espresso and chill. Pour the rum and Café Rica into a stemmed glass. Add the espresso, then slowly pour in the cream.

189

COFFEE DESSERTS

MOCHA SAUCE FOR SUNDAES
Salsa de Mocha para Helados

Melt 6 oz. of semisweet chocolate bits into 1/4 cup extra strength coffee. (For 1/4 cup coffee, brew 1 tablespoon of coffee with 1/4 water.) Add a dash of cognac.

COFFEE SYRUP
Sirope de Café

Combine 1 cup of sugar and 1 cup of extra strength coffee (2 tablespoons of coffee to 8 oz. water) and simmer for three minutes.

Use the syrup as flavoring in milk drinks and ice cream drinks, such as milk shakes.

COFFEE ICE CREAM PIE
Pie de Helado de Café

Chocolate Cookie Crust:
1 9 oz. box of chocolate cookies
6 T. melted butter
1 T. sugar

1/2 cup semi-sweet chocolate chips, melted
1 1/2 pints coffee ice cream, slightly softened

Blend the crust ingredients--chocolate cookies, sugar, and melted butter--in a food processor. Line a pie pan with the crust and spread the melted chocolate over the crust. Freeze for 5 minutes.

Spoon the ice cream into the crust, smoothing the top. Freeze until firm. Can be made up to 4 days ahead. Before serving, decorate with whipped cream or whipped topping.

Serves: 8 to 10

COFFEE AND CHOCOLATE CHEESECAKE
Cheesecake de Café y Chocolate

Crust:

1 9 oz. package chocolate cookies (*Oreos* or *Orfeas*)
2 tsp. instant espresso powder or regular instant coffee
1 T. sugar
3 oz. semi-sweet chocolate, chopped
6 T. melted butter

Filling:

32 oz. cream cheese (4 8 oz. pkgs.) at room temperature
1 1/4 cups sugar
1/4 cup coffee liquor (*Café Rica*)
1 tsp. vanilla
3 T. instant espresso powder or regular instant coffee
4 large eggs
6 oz. semi-sweet chocolate, chopped

To prepare the crust: Finely grind the cookies, sugar, and espresso powder in a food processor. Add the chocolate and chop finely. Add the butter and blend until moist crumbs form. Press the crumbs on to the bottom and sides of a 9-inch spring form pan with 2 3/4 inch sides.

Preheat the oven to 350°F. With an electric mixer beat the cream cheese and sugar in a mixing bowl until well blended. Combine the coffee liquor and espresso powder in a small sauce pan. Stir over a low heat until the coffee dissolves. Mix in the vanilla. Add the mixture to the cream cheese mixture, and beat until smooth. Then add the eggs, one at a time, beating just until combined.

Pour the filling evenly into two bowls. Melt the chocolate, and stir into one of the bowls. Pour the filling from the other bowl into the crust. Bake at 350°F for about 25 minutes, until a crust forms on the filling.

Spoon the chocolate filling over the coffee filling. Return to the oven and bake until set at the edges, but the center 2 inches still move slightly when the pan is shaken, about 30 minutes.

Transfer to a rack and cool about 20 minutes. Top with 2 oz. melted semi-sweet chocolate, and bake 10 minutes longer. Cool completely before serving. May be prepared a day ahead.

Serves: 8 to 10

MAKING NATURAL FRUIT DRINKS

 Why drink soft drinks when you can make delicious *refrescos naturales--* natural fruit drinks? These beverages can be made from the pulp of the tamarind tree or from many other fruits like *papaya, mango, guayaba, cas, mora,* or *piña.* If you have a blender and a little time, you might want to try some of the *frescos* below...

You can visit your neighborhood *feria* to find which fresh fruit is in season. The fruit will likely be half its supermarket price...and it's a fun place to shop! When you return home, pull out your blender, and you will be in business! The amount or water or milk used in each drink is dependent on your taste.

Batidos are the Central American equivalent of milkshakes. We include some healthy ones made with fresh fruit and yogurt.

NATURAL FRUIT DRINKS...

Banana: Peel and cube. Mix in blender with milk or water.

Carambola: Wash and slice. Blend with water in a blender. Strain and add sugar to taste.

Cas: Wash, then cut and scoop out the seeds. Cube and blend in blender with water to taste. Strain.

Chan: Soak the seeds in water for 1 to 2 hours. Remove seeds and add sugar to taste. OR...Put the seeds in the blender, blend with water, and strain. Add sugar or *sirope de kola* to taste.

Guanabana: Peel and remove seeds. Put the white pulp in a blender. Mix with water or milk to taste.

Limón-Naranja: Combine the juice of each in whatever proportions desired. Add water and sugar to taste.

Mango: Peel, remove the seed, and cube. Blend with water and refrigerate.

Maracuyá: Cut in half and scoop out the seeds. In a blender purée with a little water. Strain and add more water and sugar to taste.

Mora: Wash the berries, then blend with milk or water. Strain and add sugar to taste.

Piña: Peel and cube. Put in the blender, add water, and blend, then strain.

Papaya: Peel, seed, and cube. Blend with water or milk.

Sandía: Peel, remove the seeds, and cube. Mix in blender with water and strain.

Tamarindo: Peel the pods and soak in hot water for an hour or more. Squeeze pods through a strainer, reserving the amber colored water. Add sugar to taste, and serve very cold over ice.

HEALTHY TROPICAL SMOOTHIES...

Banana-Strawberry Smoothie

1 cup cracked ice   1 cup unflavored yogurt
2 cups strawberries   2 ripe bananas
1 T. honey
   Whirl all ingredients in a blender until smooth. Makes 3.

Pineapple-Banana Smoothie

1 cup cracked ice   1 cup unflavored yogurt
1 cup fresh pinapple chunks   1 banana
1 T. honey
   Whirl all ingredients in a blender until smooth. Makes 3.

Papaya-Orange Smoothie

1 cup cracked ice   1 cup unflavored yogurt
1 1/2 cups cubed papaya   1/2 cup fresh orange juice
   Whirl all ingredients in a blender until smooth. Makes 4.

SPECIAL HORCHATA MIX

2 lbs. toasted rice, raw
1/2 cup coriander seeds
1/2 cup pumpkin seeds, peeled
1/2 cup sesame seeds, lightly
   toasted

2 T. ground cinammon
2 T. toasted cashews
1/4 cup unsweeted chocolate
    powder
1 tsp. ground nutmeg

Put all seeds and nuts in the food processor and grind to a powder. Add cinnamon, chocolate, and nutmeg. Store in an air-tight glass jar until ready to use.

To make a glass, measure 3 tablespoons of the mixture to 1 tablespoon sugar for each 6 to 8 oz. water or milk. Strain the liquid after mixing and serve over ice.

ORANGE-CARROT JUICE

Crushed ice
Freshly grated nutmeg

1/2 cup fresh orange juice
1/2 cup fresh carrot juice

Fill a large glass (12 oz.) with crushed ice. Add the juices and stir well with a long-handled spoon. Grate a little nutmeg on top, and serve at once.

Serves: 1

ORANGE-BANANA DRINK

2 ripe bananas peeled and cut
1 cup vanilla ice cream

1 1/3 cups orange juice

Put all ingredients in the blender and mix until smooth.
Serves: 2

MANGO COCKTAIL

2 cups fresh mango, cubed
1/8 cup sugar, or to taste
2 cups water

2 cups fresh orange juice
1/4 cup fresh lime juice

Combine all the ingredients in a blender, mixing at high speed for about two minutes. Pour through a strainer into a pitcher. Serve over ice.

Makes: 1 pitcher

STRAWBERRY BATIDO

12 strawberries, stems removed
2 T. sugar, or to taste

1 1/2 cups cold milk
1/2 cup crushed ice

Mix ingredients in a blender and serve.
Serves: 2

BANANA-STRAWBERRY BATIDO

1 cup hulled strawberries, plus
  2 large berries for garnish
1 ripe banana
1 T. sweetened condensed milk

1 to 2 T. sugar, or to taste
1 T. lime juice, or to taste
1 1/2 cups crushed ice

Combine all of the ingredients except the strawberry garnish in a blender, and purée until smooth. Taste for sweetness, adding sugar or lime juice as necessary. Pour the *batidos* into tall glasses and garnish each with a strawberry.
Serves: 2
The same recipe can be made with 1 cup of diced watermelon and 1 cup of diced papaya.

PINEAPPLE-MINT BATIDO

1 1/2 cups diced fresh pineapple
1/3 cup canned sweetened
  coconut cream

1 1/2 cups crushed ice
1/4 cup fresh mint leaves, or
  1 1/2 tsp. dried mint with
  2 sprigs for garnish

Combine all of the ingredients except the garnish in a blender, and purée until smooth. Pour the *batidos* into tall glasses and garnish each with a sprig of mint.
Serves: 2

FRUIT PUNCH

1 cup papaya, peeled and cubed
1/2 cup pineapple, peeled and
  cubed
1 ripe banana

2 cups fresh orange juice
10 strawberries, cleaned
  and stemed
1/2 cup melon (optional)

Blend all the ingredients in the blender. If too thick, you can thin the mixture with water or additional orange juice.
Serves: 4 to 6

ALCOHOLIC BEVERAGES

A wide variety of alcohol is available in Costa Rica. The cheapest "hard stuff" is *guaro*. It's distilled sugar cane fire water with a pungent taste. It is certainly not the thing you would want to order in a refined restaurant nor serve to honored guests in your home, but if you want a "*sabor tico*", you should try it!

Rum, vodka, and gin are distilled locally, thus they can be purchased for a good price, while scotch and imported liquors will cost you an "arm and a leg". Tequila, unfortunately, is imported so don't expect to pay the same prices you do in Mexico. There are some fine Costa Rican liquors, such as *Café Rica*, a coffee liquor, and *Golden Cream*, a beverage lovers of Bailey's Irish Cream will enjoy. Both are made by Salicsa, S.A. which also makes a tasty, sweet orange liquor.

Wines are a disappointment in Costa Rica. With the exception of some poor quality fruit wines, all wines are imported. Wines do not store well in this climate, so, as a result, they can be acidic and lack the smoothness of good European and California wines. Also, many wines found in Costa Rica are not dry enough to suit some tastes. The bulk of Costa Rica's wines come from Chile...Chilean *Concha y Toro* seems to be the brand almost universally used as a house wine in restaurants. There are some fairly good Italian imports which are favorably priced. They are served in some Italian restaurants and can be purchased at upscale supermarkets like Automercado, Yaohan, Saretto, and San José 2000 and Santa Ana 2000. By the way, the latter two are Italian owned and stock many Italian imports while Saretto has the largest selection of alcoholic beverages in the country!

A lot of "inexpensive" California wines are available, and we have seen such brands as Carlo Rossi served with some flair in elegant restaurants. If you are a wine lover, you will be pleased to learn Wente Bros., Buena Vista, Hacienda, and some other higher quality

California wines have become more readily available in the last few years.

If good, reasonable wines are hard to come by, the opposite is true with beer. Imports are expensive, but the local beers are high quality and fairly priced. Imperial is the king of local beers, but a new beer, Rock Ice, has gained popularity. Bavaria and Imperial are "heavy" brews while Pilsen, Tropical, and Rock Ice are "lighter" selections. They all come in cans or 350 ml. recyclable bottles. *Cerveza cruda*, draft beer, is available at some bars and restaurants. It tastes a little green, but is quite palatable.

For end of the year holidays, its easy to buy rum and the high quality boxed eggnog (*rompope*) to serve to guests. Additionally, if you do not want to empty your wallet to purchase French or California champagne, some good sparkling wines are available. Such Spanish products as Freixenet and Codorniu are available as well as Undurraga Brut and Semi-dry from Chile.

Below are some tropical concoctions you may want to try. You will find them refreshing beverages in our tropical climate.

TICA RICA FIZZ

1 1/2 oz. *Café Rica*   4 oz. cream or milk
club soda   ice

Put the *Café Rica* and milk or cream in a tall glass. Add ice and club soda to taste. Stir to mix. If desired, top with a mint leaf.
Serves: 1

MULATA

1 1/2 oz. light rum   1 T. fresh lime juice, or to taste
3/4 oz. dark créme de cacao   1 cup ice cubes
(*Crema de Café* can be substituted)

Combine all of the ingredients in a bar shaker, cover, and shake well. Strain the Mulata into a martini glass. This drink can also be made frozen by pureeing the ingredients in a blender.
Serves: 1

HURRICANE

1/4 oz. dark rum
Splash of grenadine

4 oz. pineapple juice
2 oz. orange juice

Mix in a tall glass over ice, then stir and serve.
Serves: 1

TROPICAL DAIQUIRI

5 T. chopped papaya, strawberries,
   or any tropical fruit
1 1/2 ounces light rum
2 T. half-and-half

2 T. fresh lime juice
1 to 2 T. sugar
1 cup crushed ice
Freshly grated nutmeg

Combine all of the ingredients except the nutmeg in a blender, and blend until smooth. Pour the daiquiri into a goblet or champagne glass and lightly dust with freshly grated nutmeg.
Serves: 1

MANGO DAIQUIRI

2 cups crushed ice
1 ripe mango, peeled and cut
   (about one cup)
1/2 cup light rum

1/3 cup fresh lime juice
2 T. sugar
Lime slices for garnish

In blender combine the ice, Mango pulp, rum, lime juice, and sugar. Blend the mixture for 2 minutes at medium speed.
Serves: 4

LYCHEE COCKTAIL

1/2 cup canned lychee juice
1/2 cup gin
1/2 cup dry vermouth

Crushed ice
2 lychees, for garnish

Mix the drink ingredients with crushed ice in a blender or cocktail shaker. Divide between 2 glasses and serve with a lychee in each.
Serves: 2

GUAVA PUNCH

2 1/4 cups unsweetened   1/4 cup fresh lime juice
   pineapple juice   3/4 cup dark rum
2 cups guava juice, nectar or puree 4 dashes Angostura bitters

Mix all the ingredients and chill well. Serve on the rocks in tall chilled glasses. Garnish with chunks and slices of tropical fruit.
   Serves: 5

MONKEY'S TAIL PUNCH

6 cinnamon sticks   1 cup of powdered instant
1 1/2 tsp. grated nutmeg   coffee
4 quarts milk   1 to 1 1/2 bottles guaro
3/4 lb. sugar   (Cacique brand)
4 egg yolks   2 cups boiling water for
                                          dissolving instant coffee

Boil the milk with the spices and sugar. Beat the egg yolks. Reduce the burner to a medium heat and add the beaten yolks. Simmer the mixture for about 10 to 15 minutes, stirring constantly. Remove from the heat and cool.
   Dissolve the coffee in two cups of boiling water and cool. When cooled, add the guaro to the coffee, then mix with the milk mixture.
   Strain and refrigerate for a least 2 days before serving.
   Makes: 24 servings

GRINGO SANGRIA

1 bottle (750 ml.) dry red wine   1 lime, thinly sliced & seeded
1/4 cup (packed) light brown sugar   2 carambolas, thinly sliced
4 cinnamon sticks, 2 inches each   1 mango, peeled, sliced, and
1 cup fresh orange juice   diced
1 orange, thinly sliced & seeded   1 atemoya, peeled, seeded, &
16 oz. club soda or 7-Up   diced, or other exotic fruit

Combine the wine, brown sugar, and cinnamon sticks in a large pitcher or a punch bowl. Stir with a wooden spoon until the sugar dissolves. Stir in the orange juice and fruits. (The sangria can be prepared up to 30 minutes ahead to this stage. In fact, it will taste richer if you let the fruit macerate for 30 minutes.)
   Just before serving, stir in the club soda. Correct the flavoring, adding sugar or orange juice to taste.
   Serves: 8

OVEN TEMPERATURE CONVERSION TABLE

Fahrenheit and Centigrade

Fahrenheit	Centigrade	Temperature
200	93	
212	100	
221	105	
225	107	Very Slow
230	110	
250	121	
275	135	
284	140	Slow
300	149	
302	150	
320	160	
325	163	
350	177	Moderate
356	180	
375	190	
390	200	
400	205	
410	210	Hot
425	218	
428	220	
437	225	
450	232	
475	246	Very Hot
500	260	

To convert Fahrenheit to Centigrade:
Subtract 32, multiply by 5, and divide by 9.

To convert Centigrade to Fahrenheit:
Multiply by 9, divide by 5, and add 32.

MEASUREMENTS AND METRIC EQUIVALENTS

GRAM-OUNCE EQUIVALENTS...

Grams	Ounces	Grams	Ounces
25	0.85	85	3.0
30	1.0	100	3.5
50	1.75	125	4.4
75	2.63	150	5.25

CUP-DECILITER EQUIVALENTS...

Cups	Deciliters	Cups	Deciliters
1/4	0.56	1 1/4	2.83
1/3	0.75	1 1/3	3.0
1/2	1.13	1 1/2	3.4
2/3	1.5	1 2/3	3.75
3/4	1.68	1 3/4	4.0
1	2.27	2	4.5

1 deciliter equals 6 2/3 tablespoons
1 liter = 4 1/3 cups = 67.3 oz

APPROXIMATE METRIC EQUIVALENTS...
1 tsp. (teaspoon) = 1/6 oz. = 5 grams
1 T. (tablespoon) = 1/2 oz. = 15 grams
1 cup (16 tablespoons) = 8 oz. = 227 grams
2 cups (1 pint) = 16 oz. (1 pound) = 454 grams
4 cups (1 quart) = 32 oz. = 907 grams
1 quart = 1.057 liters
1 cup plus 1 T. = 8.5 Oz = 1/4 liter (250 grams)
4 1/3 cups = 2.2 pounds = 1 kilo (1000 grams)

FORMULAS TO CONVERT MEASUREMENTS...

To Convert	Multiply	By
Ounces to grams	Ounces	28.35
Grams to ounces	Grams	0.035
Liters to quarts	Liters	0.95
Quarts to liters	Quarts	1.057

201

EQUIVALENTS FOR AMERICAN MEASUREMENTS...
3 teaspoons (tsp.) = 1 tablespoon (T.)
4 tablespoons = 1/4 cup
5 1/3 tablespoons = 1/3 cup
8 tablespoons = 1/2 cup
16 tablespoons = 1 cup or 8 ounces
1 cup = 8 fluid ounces = 1/2 pint
2 cups = 1 pint
4 cups = 1 quart
4 quarts = 1 gallon

EMERGENCY SUBSTITUTIONS...
These will be especially useful to Central American residents!
1 square chocolate = 3 tablespoons cocoa + 1 tablespoon butter
1 tablespoon cornstarch (for thickening) = 2 tablespoons flour
1 cup buttermilk = 1 cup yogurt
1 cup milk = 1/2 cup evaporated milk + 1/2 cup water
1 cup sour milk = 1 cup milk + 1 tablespoon lime juice or vineger
1 cup cake or pastry flour = 1 cup all-purpose flour less 2 T.
1 teaspoon baking powder = 1/4 teaspoon baking soda +
        1/2 teaspoon cream of tartar
1 cup sugar = 1 cup honey (use 1/4 cup less liquid in a recipe)
1 cup brown sugar = 1 cup granulated sugar
1 cup oil = 1/2 pound butter or margarine
1 tablespoon prepared mustard = 1 teaspoon dry mustard
1 clove garlic = 1/8 teaspoon garlic powder

HERBS...
1 teaspoon dried = 1 tablespoon fresh

PASTA AND RICE EQUIVALENTS...
Macaroni: 1 cup uncooked = 2 1/2 cups cooked
Noodles: 1 cup uncooked = 2 cups cooked
Spaghetti: 8 ounces uncooked = 4 cups cooked
Rice: 1 cup = 3 cups cooked

DAIRY EQUIVALENTS...
Cheese: 4 ounces = 1 cup shredded
        1 pound = 4 cups shredded
Butter: 1 stick = 1/2 cup
        4 sticks = 2 cups = 1 pound

Sources: • Cook's Chart from CORNING, USA
        • Conversion Tables in *Mastering the Art of French
        Cooking* by Child, Bertholle, and Beck

TYPICAL COSTA RICAN DISHES
AND FOOD PRODUCTS

 When dining in a restaurant or a soda which serves *comidas típicas*, you may come across some of the following items on the menu. Most of these foods are Costa Rican, but some have their origin in other Central American countries. We list here some of the foods not given attention elsewhere in our guide.

Agua Dulce: Sugar cane juice, water sweeted with raw sugar.

Albóndigas: Hispanic meatballs.

Arepa: A cormeal dish, Colombian in origin, that's a cross between polenta and a pancake.

Arreglados: Sandwiches stuffed with beef, cheese, or chicken, served on a tasty, but somewhat greasy bun.

Arroz con Camarones: A basic rice dish with small shrimp and seasonings.

Arroz con Pollo: A basic rice dish with pieces of chicken and seasonings.

Bocas: Tid-bits served in bars with your drinks.

Café con Leche: Coffee served with milk.

Cajetas de Leche: Bars of fudge candy made with boiled milk and sugar, sometimes filled with pieces of dried fruit.

Casado: A meal with a piece of meat, chicken, or fish "married" to rice and beans, a cabbage salad, and often fried plantains.

Ceviche: Chopped raw seafood marinated in lime juice and prepared with minced onion, red pepper, and cilantro. Usually made with sea bass or various seafoods. Served chilled.

Chilasquiles: Tortillas stuffed with meat.

Elote Asado: Roasted corn on the cob.

Empanadas: Pastry turnovers stuffed with beans, cheese, meat, or chicken.

Escabeche: Foods which have been pickled.

Ensalada de Frutas: A salad made with pieces of fresh tropical fruit, usually eaten as a dessert and sometimes served with ice cream or chunks of jello.

Ensalada de Repollo: Shreded cabbage salad...the Costa Rica equivalent of coleslaw!

Galletas: Crackers or cookies.

Gallos: Tortilla sandwiches stuffed with beans, cheese, or meat.

Guacamole: A dip made from mashed avocados seasoned with onion, cilantro, spices, and sometimes chopped tomato.

Guiso de Maíz: Fresh corn stew.

Horchata: A sweet drink made from puréed rice with cinnamon and sugar and mixed with water.

Masamorra: Corn pudding.

Melcochas: Candies made from raw sugar.

Milanes: Small, foil-wrapped pure chocolate candies.

Olla de Carne: Literally, "pot of meat"...a hearty soup similar to a stew made with chunks of meat and vegetables such as corn, yuca, chayote, carrots, and potatoes.

Palomitas de Maíz: Popcorn...literally means "little doves".

Pañuelos: A type of pastry. Literally means "handkerchief".

Picadillo: A side dish of chopped vegetables, such as green beans, chayote, or potatoes, seasoned with ground meat and spices.

Quesadillas: Tortilla stuffed with cheese and sometimes chopped chiles...served grilled to melt the cheese.

Queque seco: Pound cake.

Sopa de Mondongo: A hearty soup made from tripe and vegetables.

Sopa de Tortillas: A chicken broth soup filled with vegetables and crisp pieces of tortilla.

Sopa Negra: A soup made from black bean gravy with vegetables and hard-boiled egg added.

Tacos: Tico style tacos differ from Mexican style tacos since they are rolled and topped with cabbage and sometimes barbeque sauce. They are not spicy, but you can add hot sauce!

Tapa Dulce: Raw brown sugar, sold in large solid chunks. Can be used in recipes calling for brown sugar.

Tayuyas: A Guanacastecan speciality...tortillas stuffed with cheese or beans.

Torta: A type of bread filled with meat and vegetables.

Torta Chilena: A multi-layered cake with sweet milk filling.

Tortilla: Refers to either an omelette or a thin pancake, made of flour or corn, used in place of bread with meals.

SPANISH TERMS
FOR FOOD PREPARATION

 The following list of terms will be useful when ordering in a restaurant, reading labels in the supermarket, or reading cooking instructions from a recipe written in Spanish.

ENGLISH	SPANISH
Seasoning, temperature...	
hot (temperature)	caliente
cold	frío
hot (spicy)	picante
mild, bland	suave, blando
Taste...	
bitter	amargo
dry	seco
salty	salado
sour	agrio
sweet	dulce
Ripeness...	
hard	duro
ripe	maduro, madura
soft	suave, suavecito
Thickness...	
thick	espeso
thin	ralo
Sizes and shapes...	
loaf	barra, hogaza, bollo
pieces	pedazos
roll	rollo
slices	rebanadas
stick	barra
Degree of doneness...	
medium rare	término medio
rare	poco cocido
raw, under-cooked	crudo
well done	bien cocido

How cooked...

baked	al horno
barbecued	barbacoa
brochete	en alambre
broiled	a la plancha
charbroiled	churrasco
charcoal grilled	a las brasas
grilled	a la parrilla
grilled over charcoal	al carbón
grilled over wood	a la leña
roasted	asado
smoked	ahumado
steamed	al vapor

How prepared...

baked	horneado
blended	mesclado
boiled	hervido
breaded	milanesa, empanizado
diced, minced, chopped	picado
fried	frito
grated	gratinado, rallado
marinated	marinado
mashed	majado
mixed	mixto
poached	escalfado
purée	puré
sautéed	salteado
sliced	rebanado
stewed	estofado, guisado, sudada
stuffed	relleno
whipped, beaten	batido

Your eggs...

eggs "over easy"	huevos volteados
fried eggs	huevos fritos
hard boiled eggs	huevos duros
Mexican style eggs	huevos rancheros
poached eggs	huevos pochés
scrambled eggs	huevos revueltos
soft boiled eggs	huevos tibios

These are very useful words to know when dining in a restaurant....

to share	para compartir
to take out	para llevar

SPANISH NAMES FOR COMMON
NORTH AMERICAN FOODS

 This English/Spanish list of foods is designed to help English speakers identify products in markets and make menu selections in restaurants. Since most of the items listed will likely be known to speakers of English, descriptions have not been included. The tropical fruits and vegetables featured in the heart of our guide are not included on this list.

BEVERAGES

alcoholic drink	trago
beer	cerveza
cider	sidra
juice	jugo
lemonade	limónada
milk	leche
milkshake	batido
mineral water	agua mineral
natural drinks	refrescos naturales
sodas	gaseosas
tap beer	cerveza de barril
tea	té
wine	vino

CONDIMENTS AND SAUCES

dressing	aderezo
honey	miel
jam	mermelada
jelly	jalea
ketchup	salsa de tomate
mayonnaise	mayonesa
molasses	melaza
mustard	mostaza
oil	aceite
olive oil	aceite de oliva
seasoner	sazonador
soy sauce	salsa de soya
syrup	jarabe
worcestershire sauce	salsa inglesa

DAIRY PRODUCTS

butter	mantequilla
cheese	queso
cream	crema
egg yolk	yema de huevo
eggs	huevos
ice cream	helado
lard	manteca
margarine	margarina
milk	leche
sour cream	natilla
yogurt	yogurt

FRUITS

apple	manzana
apricot	albaricoque
blackberry	mora
blueberry	arándano azul
cherry	cereza
cranberry	arándano agrio
currant	grosella
date	dátil
fig	higo
grape	uva
grapefruit	toronja
manderin orange	manderina
melon	melón
nectarine	nectarina
peach	melocotón, durazno
pear	pera
plum	ciruela
pomegranate	granado
prune	ciruela
raisin	pasa
raspberry	frambuesa
strawberry	fresa
tangerine	tangerina
watermelon	sandía

NUTS

almonds	almendras
cashew	marañon
chestnut	castaña
hazelnut	avellana
nuts	nueces
peanuts	mani
pecans	pecanas

pine nuts	piñones
walnuts	nogales

SPICES

allspice	pimienta gorda
anise	anís
basil	albahaca
bay leaf	laurel
black pepper	pimienta negra
capers	alcaparras
cardamom	cardamomo
chile powder	chile molido
cinnamon	canela
cloves	clavos de olor
cream of tartar	cremor tártaro
cumin	comino
curry powder	polvo de curry
dill	eneldo
garlic	ajo
ginger	jengibre
marjoram	mejorana
mint	menta
MSG	ajinomoto
nutmeg	nuez moscada
oregano	orégano
paprika	pimentón dulce
parsley	perejil
pepper (black)	pimienta negra
pepper (white)	pimienta blanca
poppy seeds	semillas de amapola
rosemary	romero
saffron	azafrán
sage	salvia
salt	sal
savory	ajedrea
sesame	ajonjolí
sesame seeds	semillas de ajonjolí
tarragon	estragón
thyme	tomillo
turmeric	cúrcuma
vanilla	vainilla

SWEETS

biscuit	galleta
cake	pastel, torta, queque
candy	dulce, confitura, bombón

cookie	galleta
doughnut	churro
jello	gelatina
pie	pie
pudding	budín
sponge cake	bizcocho
tart	tarta

VEGETABLES

alfalfa sprouts	alfalfa
artichoke	alcachofa
asparagus	espárragos
bean sprouts	nacidos
beets	remolachas
broccoli	brocoli
brussel sprouts	col de Bruselas
cabbage	repollo
carrot	zanahoria
cauliflower	coliflor
celery	apio
chard	acelga
chicory	achicoria
cucumber	pepino
eggplant	berenjena
endive	escarola
fennel	hinojo
green beans	vainicas
leeks	puerro
lentils	lentejas
lettuce	lechuga
lima beans	habas de lima
mushrooms	hongos
onion	cebolla
parsnip	chirivia
peas	guisantes, petit pois
potato	papa
radish	rábano
red cabbage	col morado
soybean	soya
spinach	espinaca
turnip	nabo
watercress	berro
yam	ñame
zucchini	calabacín

MISCELLANEOUS

baking powder	polvo de hornear
baking soda	bicarbonato sódico
barley	cebada
bread	pan
corn flour	masa
cornstarch	maicena
flour	harina
gravy	salsa
noodles	fideos
oatmeal	avena
olives	aceitunas
pickles	pepinillos
spaghetti	espagueti
sugar	azúcar
wheat germ	germen de trigo
wheat	trigo
yeast	levadura

REFERENCES

 The following were utilized in the writing of our guide either as recipe sources or as text information resources.

WRITTEN RESOURCES...

A Gourmet's Guide--Food and Drink From A to Z, John Ayto

Ayer y Hoy en la Cocina Salvadoreña, Gloria Dubois de Liebe

Cooking Caribe, Christofer Idone and Helen McEachrane

Fruits of Warm Climates, Julia F. Morton

Gourmet Magazine, Selected articles and recipes

Home Gardening in Costa Rica, Ed Bernhardt

Joy of Cooking, Irma S. Rombauer and Marion Rombauer Becker

Living in Costa Rica, The US Mission Association

Miami Spice, Steven Raichlen

Sunset Magazine, Selected articles and recipes

The New Basics Cookbook, Julee Rosso and Sheila Lukins

The New Key to Costa Rica, Beatrice Blake and Anne Becher

The Silver Palate Cookbook, Julee Rosso and Sheila Lukins

Tico Times Selected "Plants at a Glance" and "Nutrition News" columns. "What is it?" columns from the newspaper's predecessor.

ELECTRONIC RESOURCES...

Epicurious Dictionary, Web Site: www.epicurious.com

Grolier Multimedia Encyclopedia, CD ROM from Mindscape

Wegmans Food Market, Web Site: www.wegmans.com

RECIPE INDEX

For your convenience we have indexed by type the recipes in our guide.

All **beverages** appear in three sections— Coffee Drinks, Natural Fruit Drinks, and Alcoholic Beverages; thus, they are not indexed.

SALADS

SOUPS

SIDE DISHES

ENTREES

DESSERTS

NOTES

NOTES

NOTES

NOTES

NOTES